Presented to:

_____

By:

_____

On this date:

_____

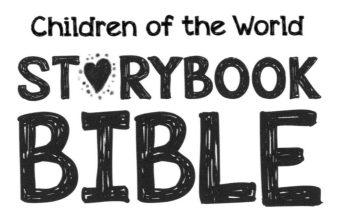

Children of the World

ST♥RYBOOK
BIBLE

Children of the World

ST♥RYBOOK BIBLE

WITH ILLUSTRATIONS BY
CHILDREN FROM AROUND THE GLOBE

Art by
ELOA
Age 13,
BRAZIL

Written by Linda Washington

Worthy **kids**
ideals

ISBN-13: 978-1-945470-27-1

Published by WorthyKids/Ideals, an imprint of Worthy Publishing Group, a division of Worthy Media, Inc., in association with Museum of the Bible.

m
museum of the Bible
BOOKS

Copyright © 2017 by Museum of the Bible Books
409 3rd St. SW
Washington, D.C. 20024-4706
Museum of the Bible is an innovative, global, educational institution whose purpose is to invite all people to engage with the history, narrative, and impact of the Bible.

Library of Congress CIP data is on file

Unless otherwise indicated, scripture quotations are from the ESV® Bible (*The Holy Bible, English Standard Version®*), copyright © 2001 by Crossway, a publishing ministry of Good News Publishers. Used by permission. All rights reserved.

Cover design by Georgina Chidlow
Produced with the assistance of Hudson Bible (www.HudsonBible.com)
Cover image by Shutterstock

Printed and bound in the U.S.A.
SHER_Aug17_1

Special thanks to all of the young artists and others who helped make this book possible.

ABOUT THE BOOK

What makes a story fun or interesting? Not knowing what will happen next? Unexpected turns? Funny events? Scary or heroic characters? The Bible is filled with stories with all of these things. And while this book can't hold *all* of the stories in the Bible, it has one hundred stories—some you may know and some that may be new to you.

The Children of the World Storybook Bible is different from other books of Bible stories you may have seen. The art in this book was drawn by kids from around the world! Real kids from almost fifty countries drew pictures of their favorite Bible stories. Then we collected the drawings and put them in this book. (Read more about this on page 231.)

As you turn the pages, you'll see this colorful art by kids, and you'll read about daring escapes, like when the Israelites crossed the Red Sea, and battles between good and evil, like when David faced the giant Goliath with only his sling. You'll read about the birth of Jesus and the amazing miracles he performed. You'll find stories about evil men like Haman, who tried to kill all the Jewish people—and brave Queen Esther, who tricked Haman and saved them. There are stories of kings, like David and Saul, and stories about common people, like Zacchaeus, a tax collector who climbed a tree to see Jesus. You'll quickly discover that the Bible is filled with fascinating stories.

We invite you to turn the page and begin your reading adventure. You may even be inspired to create some drawings of your own!

TABLE of CONTENTS

Art by
CINDY
Age 11,
CANADA

Art by
HANNA
Age 8,
CHINA

Art by
SANDRA
Age 12,
GEORGIA

Art by ANDRÉS
Age 12, GUATEMALA

NEW TESTAMENT 145

Art by
SARETH
Age 12,
BOLIVIA

Art by
JOHN MARK
Age 13,
PHILIPPINES

OLD TESTAMENT

GOD
Creates the
WORLD

Genesis 1:1–2:24

In the beginning, there was only God. Then God created the world. At first, the world was empty. There was no sky, no land, no animals, no people. There was just darkness and water.

God said, "Let there be light." And light appeared. God called the light "day." He called the darkness "night." This was the first day.

Next, God separated the water.

Now there was water above the earth and water on the earth and a space in the middle. God called this middle space the "sky." This was the second day.

On the third day, God gathered all the water on earth and called the water the "seas." He made dry land appear, and he called the land "earth." He made trees and plants to grow on the earth. The trees and plants would produce fruit and seeds to make more trees and plants. God's creation was good.

Next, God made the sun and the moon and the stars. The sun provided light for the day. The moon and stars provided light for the night. This was the fourth day.

Art by
SHREYA
Age 9,
INDIA

3

God made all the animals in the sea and all the
creatures in the sky. Whales and fish and turtles swam.
Birds of all colors flew. God blessed his creation. This was
the fifth day.

On the sixth day, God made animals to run and hop and crawl
on the land. He made lions and bears, dogs and cats, mice and
bunnies. His creation was good.

Then God said, "Let us make man in our image, after our
likeness." He made a man called Adam. Then he made a woman

4

called Eve. God blessed his creation. And he put
humans in charge of caring for all the creatures on
the earth.

On the seventh day God rested from all his work. Everything
he made was very good.

ADAM and EVE DISOBEY GOD

Genesis 2:8–17, 3:1–24

God made a beautiful garden in Eden for Adam and Eve to live in. He gave them one important rule to follow. They could eat from any tree in the garden except the tree of the knowledge of good and evil.

One day, a sneaky snake said to Eve, "Did God actually say, 'You shall not eat of any tree in the garden'?"

Eve told the snake that God said they could eat from any tree except the one tree in the middle of the garden.

The snake told Eve that if she ate the fruit, she would be like God, and she would know about good and evil. So Eve ate the fruit and then gave some to Adam. He ate it too.

After they ate the fruit, Adam and Eve knew they had done something wrong. They were scared. When they heard God walking in the garden, they hid from him. God called out, "Where are you?"

Art by
YUKA
Age 11,
JAPAN

Adam told God that he was hiding.

"Did you eat fruit from the tree I told you not to eat?" asked God.

Adam blamed Eve for what happened. Eve blamed the snake. Then God sent Adam and Eve away from the garden.

CAIN and ABEL

Genesis 4:1–16

After they left the garden of Eden, Adam and Eve had two sons. Their names were Cain and Abel. Cain, the older son, was a farmer who grew crops. Abel was a shepherd who watched over sheep.

One day, Cain and Abel decided to give gifts to God. Their gifts were called offerings. Abel gave God the first sheep born from his flock. Cain gave God some of the food he had grown.

God was pleased with Abel and his gift, but he was not pleased with Cain and his gift.

Art by
HARENA
Age 10,
MADAGASCAR

This made Cain angry. He became so angry that he killed Abel!

God asked Cain, "Where is Abel your brother?" Cain lied and said he didn't know, but God knew what Cain had done. He told Cain that no matter how hard he worked, the land would no longer grow crops for him. Instead, Cain would have to leave his home and spend the rest of his life wandering the earth.

NOAH
and the
FLOOD

Genesis 6:9–9:17

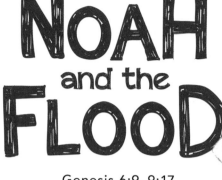

In Noah's time, people did whatever they pleased. They were not good or honest.

God saw everything they did. Their behavior made him sad and angry. He decided to send a flood to make the world new again.

Noah was a good man and lived in a way that pleased God. God told Noah that he would be sending a flood. God said he would save Noah's family and two of every kind of animal from the flood.

First, Noah had to build a huge boat called an ark. Noah built the ark just as God told him to. Then God sent animals to the ark two by two, one male and one female.

He sent every kind of animal—apes and
aardvarks, ducks and deer, lions and lemurs.
Some animals came in seven pairs.

   When they were all inside, God closed the door of the ark.
Then God sent the flood just as he told Noah he would. Rain fell
from the sky for forty days and nights. Soon the ark floated
on water higher than the mountains! Noah, his family,
and the animals were safe and
dry inside the ark.

After many days
of floating on water,
the ark landed
on a mountain.

But there was still water all around the ark. More days passed. Noah sent a raven and a dove to find dry land, but the birds returned when they couldn't find any.

Noah waited a week and sent the dove out again. This time the dove brought back a branch from an olive tree. Noah waited another week and then sent the dove out a third time. This time the dove did not return. That meant the bird had found land!

More than a year after going into the ark, Noah's family and the animals stepped out onto dry land.

God promised he would never again destroy all living things on earth with a flood. He placed a rainbow in the sky as a reminder of his promise.

Art by
MAMIKINA
Age 9,
RUSSIA

The TOWER of BABEL

Genesis 11:1–9

Many years passed after the great flood. There were lots of people on the earth. Everyone spoke the same language.

A group of people decided to build a city. They said, "Let's build ourselves a city with a tower that reaches to the heavens. And let us make a name for ourselves." They wanted to stay together instead of scattering over the earth.

But God saw their city and their tower. He said, "This is only the beginning of what they will do."

So God mixed up their language, and the people couldn't understand one another! They couldn't work together anymore. God sent the people to live in different parts of the world. Their city was left unfinished, and it was called Babel.

Art by
REHMA
Age 12,
PAKISTAN

Art by
ZAFAR
Age 12,
UNITED ARAB
EMIRATES

A PROMISE for ABRAM

Genesis 12:1–9, 15:1–21, 17:1–16

A man named Abram lived in a land called Haran. God told Abram, "Leave your country and go to the land that I will show you."

Abram didn't know where God would lead him, but he obeyed God. He went with his wife, Sarai, and his nephew Lot to the land where God told them to go.

One day, God spoke to Abram in a dream. "Don't be afraid, Abram," said God. Then God promised to give Abram many blessings.

Later God told Abram that he and Sarai would have a son. But Abram and Sarai had no children, and they were

16

very old. It didn't seem possible that they could have their own children.

God told Abram to look up at the sky. Abram saw many, many stars. God promised that Abram would have as many descendants as there are stars in the sky. Abram believed God.

God changed Abram's name to Abraham, which means "father of many." Sarai's name changed to Sarah, which means "princess."

17

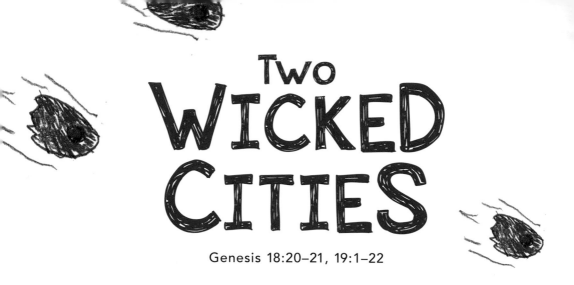

Two WICKED CITIES

Genesis 18:20–21, 19:1–22

The people living in the cities of Sodom and Gomorrah were doing evil things. So God sent two angels to see if there was anyone good living in the two cities.

The angels went to Sodom, where Abraham's nephew Lot lived. Lot invited them to his house. That night, wicked men tried to break into Lot's house. They wanted to harm the angels, but the angels blinded the men.

The angels knew that God would destroy the evil cities. They helped rescue Lot and his family before the city was destroyed. The angels led Lot, his wife, and their two daughters out of the city. One of the angels warned them, "Run for your life. Don't look back or stop anywhere."

18

Fire fell from the sky on Sodom and Gomorrah. The two cities and the wicked people were destroyed. Lot and his daughters safely escaped, but his wife did not. She disobeyed the angels' instructions and looked back at the cities. When she did, something strange happened. She turned into a pillar of salt.

Art by
FULGENT
Age 9,
MALAYSIA

ABRAHAM
Offers
ISAAC

Genesis 21:1–7, 22:1–14

God had promised Abraham and Sarah a son. But Abraham was one hundred years old. His wife, Sarah, was ninety. Could this really happen? Yes! God kept his promise, and Sarah had a baby boy they named Isaac. They loved their son very much.

One day, God told Abraham, "Take your son and go to the land of Moriah. Offer him there as a burnt offering."

Usually a burnt offering was an animal, such as a lamb. The animal was killed and burned on an altar. But instead of an animal, Isaac would be the offering!

Abraham obeyed God. He took Isaac to a mountain God had chosen. Isaac carried wood to burn on the altar. Abraham carried a knife and some fire.

Isaac saw the fire and the wood. "But where is the lamb for a burnt offering?" he asked.

"God will provide the lamb," Abraham replied.

Abraham built an altar and then placed his son on it. He grabbed his knife. Suddenly, God's angel called out, "Abraham, Abraham! Don't touch the boy or do anything to him." God saw that Abraham truly loved God more than anything or anyone else, even his son.

Just then, Abraham saw a ram caught by its horns in a bush. He gave the ram as an offering to God.

JACOB
and
ESAU

Genesis 25:19–34, 27:1–29

Isaac grew up and married a woman named Rebekah. They had twin sons. Esau was born first. He was red and hairy. Jacob was born second. His skin was smooth. The brothers grew up to be very different. Esau became a hunter, while Jacob liked staying at home. Isaac loved Esau best, but Rebekah loved Jacob best. One day, Esau came home from hunting and was very hungry.

He smelled a delicious stew that Jacob had made. He asked his brother for some of the stew.

"Sell me your birthright," said Jacob. A birthright was an important promise. It meant the oldest son would inherit most of what their father owned. Esau was tired and hungry. He really wanted the stew, so he sold Jacob his birthright.

Now their father had become old and blind. One day he asked Esau to go and make a meal for him. Isaac planned to give Esau his blessing after Esau came back with the meal.

Rebekah wanted Jacob to get the blessing instead. While Esau was hunting, she made food for Jacob to give to his father. Jacob dressed up in Esau's clothes and wore animal skins on his arms. Isaac tasted the meal. He felt his son's hairy arms. The trick worked. Isaac gave Esau's blessing to Jacob.

Art by
LEA
Age 10,
SERBIA

23

JACOB'S DREAM

Genesis 27:41–46, 28:1–5, 10–22

Jacob had tricked his father, and now Jacob had the blessing meant for his twin brother, Esau. This made Esau so angry he wanted to kill Jacob. But their mother had a plan to help Jacob escape.

Jacob would go to the land of Haran. He would live with his uncle Laban and find a wife there.

Haran was far away. Jacob traveled for many days. One night, he slept outside,

using a stone for a pillow. When he fell asleep, he had a strange dream. He saw a tall ladder that reached from the earth all the way to heaven. Angels were going up and down the ladder.

God spoke to Jacob in the dream. "I am the LORD, the God of Abraham your father and the God of Isaac." God promised to give Jacob and his children the land where Jacob had slept. God also promised to be with Jacob wherever he would go.

Jacob woke up and said, "The LORD is in this place." He set up his stone pillow as a marker and poured oil over it. He named the place Bethel, which means "the house of God." Then Jacob made a promise. He said, "If God will be with me, the LORD shall be my God."

JACOB
Wrestles with
GoD

Genesis 32:1–33:4

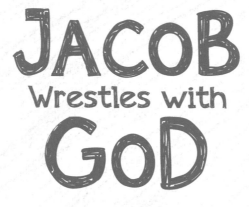

J acob got married in Haran and had many children. Now it was time to go back to his home. But he was afraid of one thing. What if his brother, Esau, was still angry with him? On the long journey home, Jacob sent messengers ahead. One day, they reported that Esau was on his way with four hundred men! Jacob was afraid. To keep his family safe, Jacob sent them to the other side of a stream while he stayed behind.

Now Jacob was all alone—or so he thought. A man began to wrestle with him. It wasn't Esau. Jacob didn't know who it was. They wrestled all night, but Jacob refused to let go. The man touched Jacob's hip, hurting him.

In the morning, the man told Jacob to let him go.

"I won't let you go unless you bless me," Jacob replied.

The man said, "You will no longer be called Jacob. You will be called Israel." The man gave Jacob the name Israel because he had wrestled with God.

Jacob said, "I have seen God face to face, but my life has been saved."

After that, Israel went to meet his brother. Esau was happy to see him. The two brothers hugged and cried.

JOSEPH
and His
BROTHERS

Genesis 37, 39–45

Jacob had twelve sons. Joseph was his favorite. Jacob gave Joseph a very fancy coat, and this made his older brothers jealous. Then Joseph had two strange dreams. In the dreams, his brothers bowed down to him. When Joseph told his brothers about the dreams, they really hated him!

The brothers decided to kill Joseph. But Reuben, the oldest brother, convinced them to throw Joseph into an empty pit instead. He planned to sneak back and rescue Joseph later, but Reuben never got the chance. While he was away, his brothers sold Joseph as a slave.

Art by
JANE
Age 10,
CANADA

They told their father
that Joseph was killed by a wild animal.

So Joseph was taken to Egypt as a slave.
There, an officer named Potiphar bought Joseph.
At first, Potiphar was pleased with Joseph. Joseph worked hard
and did everything well. But then Potiphar's wife told a lie about
Joseph. Potiphar was angry and put Joseph in prison. Joseph still
worked hard in prison. The jailer was pleased and put Joseph in
charge of the other prisoners.

One day, the Egyptian king, Pharaoh, put two of his household
servants in prison. One was a baker and one was a cupbearer.
While in prison, they both had dreams that they didn't understand.

Joseph explained what the dreams meant, and everything he said came true.

Later, Pharaoh had two dreams. In one dream, seven fat cows came out of the river. Seven skinny cows came after them and ate the plump cows. In the other dream, seven plump ears of grain grew on a stalk. Seven thin ears grew up and ate the plump ears. Pharaoh wondered what the dreams meant.

The cupbearer remembered Joseph from prison. He told Pharaoh that he knew a man who understood dreams.

Pharaoh called for Joseph and told him the dreams. God helped Joseph understand what they meant. Joseph explained that there would be seven years of good harvests. Then there would be seven years of famine, when there would be no food. Joseph said Pharaoh should set aside grain for the bad years.

Pharaoh thought Joseph was very wise. He made Joseph second-in-command of Egypt.

Seven years later, the famine started. Crops would not grow. People became hungry. Far away, Jacob's family had no food. Jacob sent his sons—Joseph's brothers—to Egypt to buy grain.

When Joseph's brothers got to Egypt, they went to
the man in charge of grain. It was Joseph! The brothers didn't
recognize him. They bowed down to him, just like in Joseph's
dreams. Joseph said, "I am Joseph, your brother!"

The brothers were afraid Joseph would harm them. Instead,
Joseph forgave them. They all hugged and cried tears of joy.
Joseph was happy to hear his father, Jacob, was still alive. Joseph's
brothers, their families, and Jacob all moved to Egypt to live
near Joseph.

SLAVES in EGYPT

Exodus 1:1–2:10

After many years, Jacob's family grew to become a huge nation. They were called people of Israel or the Israelites, and also called Hebrews. A new king ruled over Egypt, and he didn't like that there were so many Israelites in his land. He forced the Israelites to work as slaves. He even had their baby boys killed.

An Israelite couple had a newborn son. The woman hid her son so he wouldn't be killed. When he became too big to hide,

she made a basket and placed her son inside it. She put the basket at the edge of the river. Miriam, the baby's sister, watched over the basket.

Soon, Pharaoh's daughter came to the river and found the basket. When she heard the baby crying, she felt sorry for him. She wanted to keep the baby.

Miriam asked, "Shall I find one of the Israelite women to nurse the child for you?"

Miriam got her mother to nurse the baby. In this way, the baby's own mother nursed and raised him until he was a little older. Then she brought him back to Pharaoh's daughter. The Egyptian princess took the baby as her own son and gave him the name Moses.

MOSES
Tries to
HELP

Exodus 2:11–25

Moses grew up in Pharaoh's family, even though he was an Israelite. Moses saw that the Egyptians mistreated his people. One day, he saw an Egyptian beating a Hebrew slave. Moses looked around to see if anyone was watching. Then he killed the Egyptian and hid the body in the sand.

The next day, Moses saw two Israelites fighting. He tried to help, but one of them asked, "Will you kill me like you killed the Egyptian?"

Moses realized that people knew what he had done! When Pharaoh found out, he wanted to kill Moses. So Moses ran away to a land called Midian. He sat down by a well.

Soon some women came to get water for their animals. A group of shepherds forced the women away from the well. Moses came to their rescue and helped them.

When the women went home, their father asked them why they had returned so early.

"An Egyptian protected us. He got water for our animals," they said.

The father invited Moses to their house. Later, Moses married Zipporah, one of the women he helped at the well.

The BURNING BUSH

Exodus 3:1–4:17

Moses stayed in the land of Midian and became a shepherd. One day, he was with his flock out in the wilderness. There, he saw a strange sight. A bush was on fire, but it did not burn up.

He heard a voice calling, "Moses, Moses!" But there was no one around.

"Here I am," Moses replied.

"Do not come near," said the voice. "Take your sandals off your feet, for you are standing on holy ground. I am the God of your father, the God of Abraham, the God of Isaac, and the God of Jacob."

It was the voice of God! Moses was afraid to look at God, so he hid his face.

God gave Moses an important job. He wanted Moses to lead the people of Israel out of Egypt so they would no longer be slaves. Moses would have to talk to Pharaoh, the king of Egypt.

Moses asked God what he should tell the people of Israel. God told Moses to tell them, "I AM WHO I AM has sent me to you."

Moses didn't think people would believe him or listen to him. So God gave Moses a powerful sign. He told Moses to throw his staff on the ground. Suddenly, the staff turned into a snake! God told Moses that when this happened, the Israelites would believe the Lord had appeared to him.

Moses told God that he could not speak well and asked him to send someone else.

Then God got angry. God told Moses that his brother, Aaron, would speak for him. Moses obeyed God and went to Egypt.

Art by
AISHA
Age 12,
MAURITIUS

PLAGUES on EGYPT

Exodus 7–13

God sent Moses and Aaron to Egypt. They told Pharaoh to let God's people go out to the wilderness to worship God. Pharaoh would not listen to them, so God punished Pharaoh and the Egyptians. He sent ten plagues, or troubles, that showed his great power.

First, Aaron stretched out his hand over the Nile River. He hit the water with his staff. The water turned to blood! All over Egypt, water in ponds and cups and wells turned to blood. But Pharaoh did not let the people of Israel go.

One week later, God sent a second plague. Aaron stretched out his hand once again. This time, frogs appeared everywhere! They filled the land of Egypt. Pharaoh begged Moses and Aaron to ask God to take away the frogs. But when God let the frogs die out, Pharaoh still wouldn't let the people of Israel go.

Art by
JACO
Age 12,
SOUTH
AFRICA

39

So God sent a third plague—tiny bugs called gnats. Every speck of dust in Egypt turned into a gnat. They covered people and animals, but Pharaoh still wouldn't listen to God.

Again and again, God sent plagues on Egypt. The fourth plague was flies.

The fifth plague killed the Egyptians' animals. But Pharaoh wouldn't let the people of Israel go!

For the sixth plague, the Egyptians—and their animals—were covered in huge, painful sores called boils.

For the seventh plague, God sent a terrible hailstorm. Thunder crashed. Lightning flashed. All the trees broke. Plants were crushed. Did Pharaoh obey God this time? No.

For the eighth plague, God sent a swarm of locusts. They ate all the plants that weren't destroyed by the hail. Each time God sent a plague, he protected the people of Israel.

Art by
SUNIL
Age 12,
BANGLADESH

For the ninth plague, God sent a thick darkness over the land of Egypt. The Egyptians couldn't see anything! Pharaoh still refused to let God's people go.

God sent one last plague on Egypt. It was the worst one yet. At midnight, all the oldest sons in Egypt died. In every Egyptian home, someone died. Even Pharaoh's oldest son died. But no one died in the homes of the people of Israel. God had told the Israelites what they must do to be protected. Each Israelite family killed a lamb and put some of its blood around the door of their house. They ate the lamb that night. This was the start of a new holiday they called Passover.

Finally, Pharaoh let the people go.

CROSSING the RED SEA

Exodus 13:17–14:31

The people of Israel had been slaves in Egypt for four hundred years, but now they were free. They could leave Egypt! God's people walked across the wilderness to the Red Sea.

God showed the people the way. During the day, he went in front of the Israelites in a large pillar of cloud. At night, he went before them in a big pillar of fire so they could see where they were going.

But Pharaoh changed his mind. He wanted his slaves back. Pharaoh and his army chased after them in chariots. The people of Israel were afraid.

The people complained that Moses and Aaron had brought them out of Egypt to die in the wilderness.

"Don't be afraid," Moses told them. "The LORD will fight for you."

God told Moses to hold his staff out over the sea. When he did, the waters split apart. The people walked right across on dry land!

Soon, the Egyptian soldiers reached the sea. They saw the dry path and started to cross. God told Moses to hold out his hand over the sea. While the Egyptians were still in the middle of crossing, the waters came crashing back down. Pharaoh's army drowned in the sea. Now the Israelites were truly free.

Art by
PRAISE
Age 12,
NIGERIA

43

BREAD
from
HEAVEN

Exodus 16

God took care of the people of Israel. He rescued them from slavery in Egypt. He brought them safely across the Red Sea. Now they were in the wilderness. Water and food were hard to find. The people grumbled to Moses and Aaron.

The people remembered the food they had to eat in Egypt. They accused Moses and Aaron of bringing them to the wilderness to starve to death.

God heard everything the people said. He told Moses that he would take care of the people.

God said he would send bread from heaven in the mornings. The people should gather just enough food to eat for one day. On the sixth morning,

44

they could gather enough for two days. That way, they could rest on the seventh day.

Just as God said, small flakes covered the ground every morning. The people called the flakes "manna." They cooked it and ate it.

Some people didn't listen to God's instructions. They went out looking for manna on the seventh day, but they didn't find any. Others gathered more manna than they needed for a day, but the extra food spoiled.

God also sent birds, called quail. The people killed and ate the birds.

The people of Israel spent many years in the wilderness, but God always gave them enough to eat.

Art by
WANANGWA
Age 12,
MALAWI

45

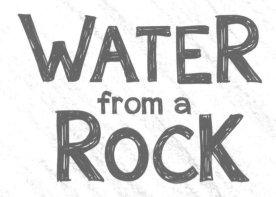

WATER from a ROCK

Exodus 17:1–7

The people of Israel were living in the wilderness. They needed food, so God sent manna and quail. They needed a place to live, so they set up a camp. They needed water to drink, but there was none!

"Give us water to drink," the people complained to Moses. "Why did you bring us up out of Egypt, to kill us and our children and our animals with thirst?"

Moses asked God for help. "What can I do with these people?"

God told Moses to go with some of the leaders to a place called Horeb. There, he would find a rock. Gold told Moses to strike the rock with his staff.

Moses obeyed God. He struck the rock, and water came out of it. Now the people had water to drink!

God spoke to Moses and gave him ten important laws called commandments. God said, "I am the LORD your God, who brought you out of Egypt."

1. **You are to have no other gods except me.**
2. **Do not worship idols.** An idol is a false god, often made of wood, metal, or stone.
3. **Do not misuse my name.**
4. **Remember the Sabbath day and keep it holy.** On the seventh day, people should rest from their work and worship God.
5. **Honor your father and mother.**
6. **Do not murder.**
7. **Do not commit adultery.** A married person should be faithful to their husband or wife.
8. **Do not steal.**
9. **Do not lie.**
10. **Do not wish for things that someone else has.**

When God finished speaking to Moses, God carved the commandments on stone tablets. He gave the tablets to Moses to share with the people.

The GOLDEN CALF

Exodus 32

Moses spent a long time on the mountain with God. The people of Israel got tired of waiting for him to return. They weren't sure if he was dead or alive.

"Make us gods to lead us," they demanded of Aaron, the brother of Moses.

"Take off your rings of gold and bring them to me," Aaron said. The people gave Aaron their earrings. He melted the gold and shaped it into a golden calf.

Aaron held a festival in honor of the golden calf. The people killed animals as offerings to the golden calf. They sang and danced and ate food to celebrate.

Up on the mountain, God knew what the people were doing. He was very angry that they were worshiping a golden calf. God told Moses that he would destroy the people. But Moses begged God to let them live.

When Moses came down from the mountain, he saw the people celebrating and worshiping the golden calf. He was so angry he threw down the stone tablets from God and broke them. Then he melted the calf, ground it into powder, and sprinkled it on the water. He made the people drink the water. God also punished the people by sending a plague, or sickness.

Later, God forgave the Israelites and gave Moses new stone tablets.

Art by
DIANA
Age 10,
MEXICO

53

The TWELVE SPIES

Numbers 13:1–14:38

God promised his people a land of their own. Now, after crossing the wilderness, the Israelites were ready to go to their new land. Moses chose twelve men to sneak into the land of Canaan and look around. He wanted to know what the cities and people were like in the land God had promised them.

The spies traveled throughout the land for forty days. They saw plenty of food, including bunches of grapes so big that it took two men to carry them. The spies also saw big, strong people living in the land.

When they returned to the people of Israel, the spies reported that the land was very good. Two of the spies—named Caleb and Joshua—wanted to take the land right away.

But the others said, "We can't go up against the people. They are stronger than we are."

The people of Israel couldn't agree on what to do. They grumbled and complained. Some wanted to return to Egypt.

God was angry that the people did not trust him. He told Moses that they would have to wander in the wilderness for forty years. Most of them would grow old and die during that time. Only Joshua, Caleb, and the children would get to enter the land God had promised them.

BALAAM'S DONKEY

Numbers 22

The people of Israel had enemies. One of them was Balak, the king of Moab. He wanted to curse the people of Israel. King Balak sent messengers to a prophet named Balaam to ask for his help.

God told Balaam not to curse the people of Israel and not to go with the king's messengers. At first, Balaam obeyed God and sent the messengers away. But King Balak sent more men to persuade Balaam to curse the people of Israel. This time, Balaam saddled his donkey and went with the king's men.

Balaam's disobedience made God angry. God sent an angel to stand in the road with a sword in his hand. Balaam couldn't see the angel. But the donkey could, and she turned off the road.

Balaam struck the donkey, forcing her to return to the road. Twice more the angel blocked

56

the road. Each time, the donkey stopped. And each time, Balaam struck her.

Then God gave the donkey the ability to speak. "What have I done to make you hit me three times?" the donkey asked.

Balaam said, "You have made me look foolish."

Then God allowed Balaam to see the angel. After that, Balaam obeyed God.

Art by
JANELLE
Age 11,
PHILIPPINES

57

RAHAB
and the
TWO SPIES

Joshua 2

After Moses died, Joshua became the new leader of the people of Israel. It was time to go into the land the LORD God had promised to them.

Joshua sent two spies into the city of Jericho. The spies went to the home of a woman named Rahab. Her house was part of the wall that surrounded the city.

When the king of Jericho found out about the two Israelite spies, he sent men to Rahab's house. "Bring out the men who are in your house," they told her.

Rahab told the king's men that the spies left. She urged them to hurry and try to catch the spies.

The king's men left Rahab's house, but they didn't find the spies. Rahab had hidden them on the roof.

Rahab told the spies that the people of Jericho were afraid of them. The people had heard how the LORD dried up the Red Sea and how he defeated the kings of other nations. Rahab knew that the LORD would give Jericho to the Israelites. She asked the spies to be kind to her, as she had been kind to them. The spies promised that when they took the city, they would save Rahab and her family.

Rahab helped the spies escape the city. She let them down from a window in her house with a rope. The spies told her to tie a scarlet cord in her window. This way, they would know which house was hers when they returned.

The spies kept their promise. They brought Rahab and her family to live with the people of Israel.

Art by
ANJALI
Age 11,
INDIA

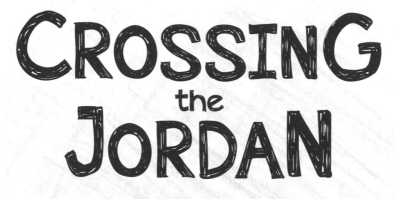

CROSSING the JORDAN

Joshua 3–4

The Israelites were now ready to enter the land the LORD God had promised to them. To get there, they had to cross the Jordan River. All the people, young and old, had to cross to the other side of the river.

The priests went first. They carried the special box that held the tablets of the Ten Commandments. The box was called the Ark of the Covenant. When the priests stepped into the Jordan River carrying the Ark, the water stopped flowing. The priests stood in the dry riverbed with the Ark while all the people walked across.

Then the LORD told Joshua to choose twelve men. Each man was to pick up a stone from the riverbed. The stones would remind them that the LORD stopped the Jordan River. Joshua set up the twelve stones in the riverbed where the priests stood.

When the people finished crossing, the priests carried the Ark to the other side. As soon as they stepped out of the riverbed, the water flowed again.

Art by
EGOR
Age 9,
BELARUS

The WALLS of JERICHO

Joshua 6:1–16

As the people of Israel moved into the land of Canaan, they needed to conquer the city of Jericho. But how would they get past the great walls around the city?

The LORD God gave Joshua important instructions. He told Joshua to march his army around the city. Some priests would carry the Ark of the Covenant. Other priests would carry trumpets. Joshua and his army would do this every day for six days. On the seventh day, they would march around the city seven times. Then the priests would blow their trumpets. All the people would shout. The LORD promised the walls around the city would fall.

The people followed the LORD's instructions. They marched around the city once a day for six days.

Art by
MARIA
Age 11,
BRAZIL

On the seventh day, they marched around it seven times. Then Joshua told the people, "Shout, for the Lord has given you the city."

Everyone shouted. The walls of Jericho crashed to the ground! The Israelites conquered the city!

Art by
MATHISHA
Age 12,
SRI LANKA

ACHAN
and the
BATTLE AT AI

Joshua 6:17–19, 7:1–8:29

The people of Israel conquered Jericho. Joshua warned them not to take anything from the city for themselves. He explained that everything in that city that was made of gold, silver, bronze, and iron would be given to the LORD.

One man didn't listen to Joshua. He took things he was not supposed to take. And the LORD knew what he had done.

Joshua led the men of Israel to fight a battle in the city of Ai. They thought they would win easily, but they lost.

Joshua didn't understand why they lost. He tore his clothes and prayed. The LORD told him that someone had taken for himself things that were meant for God. Until this disobedience was stopped, Israel would lose against their enemies.

Art by
MARINA
Age 12,
EGYPT

Joshua discovered who the thief was. His name was Achan. Achan admitted that he had taken a cloak, silver, and a bar of gold. Achan and his whole family were punished. After that, Israel won the battle at Ai.

When THE SUN Stood STILL

Joshua 10:1–28

With the LORD God on their side, the Israelites grew strong. They became friends with the people of Gibeon. This scared the king of Jerusalem. He did not want Israel and Gibeon to become more powerful than he was. So the king of Jerusalem and four other kings went to war against the city of Gibeon.

The people of Gibeon could not defeat five kings by themselves. They asked Joshua for help. The LORD told Joshua not to be afraid, because he would help him win the battle. Joshua and the army of Israel marched all night to reach Gibeon.

Suddenly, the Israelite army attacked. Joshua asked the LORD to make the sun and moon stand still during the battle. The LORD answered by making the sun stand still in the sky for a whole day.

The Israelites beat the armies of the five kings and chased them away. Then the LORD sent large hailstones down from the sky to kill any enemies who escaped. Israel won the battle!

Art by
JOSUÉ
CALEB
Age 12,
BOLIVIA

DEBORAH AND BARAK
Go to
WAR

Judges 4

After Joshua died, many people in Israel stopped worshiping God. So God allowed enemies to attack Israel again and again. One of these enemies was Jabin, the king of Canaan. His army attacked Israel with nine hundred iron chariots. They seemed unstoppable. The people of Israel asked God for help.

God had chosen special leaders, called judges, to guide Israel during this time. The judges gave the people advice and helped them fight their enemies. Deborah was one of Israel's judges. She was also a prophet who spoke for God.

Deborah called on a man named Barak. She told him that God had chosen him to

lead Israel's army against the king of Canaan. But Barak refused to go unless Deborah went with him.

"I'll go with you," replied Deborah. She told Barak that God would give them the victory over Jabin. She also told Barak that God would let a woman defeat Sisera, the leader of Jabin's army.

Barak led ten thousand soldiers against Sisera's army. God helped Israel win the battle, but Sisera escaped and hid in the tent of a woman named Jael. While he was asleep, Jael killed him with a tent peg. The words God had spoken to Deborah had come true.

Art by
ALEX
Age 11,
ITALY

GIDEON'S FLEECE

Judges 6:1–24, 36–40

The people of Israel continued to disobey God. So for seven years, God let the Midianites overpower them. The Midianites stole food and animals from the Israelites. The people of Israel had to hide in caves and had very little to eat. They cried out to God for help.

God heard them, and he sent an angel to a man named Gideon.

The angel urged Gideon to go and save Israel from the Midianites.

Gideon didn't understand. How could *he* save Israel? He was no one special. But God promised to help Gideon defeat Israel's enemies.

Gideon wanted proof that God would truly help him defeat the Midianites, so he thought of a test. Gideon placed a sheep's fleece on the ground. If he found dew on the fleece but the ground around it was dry, he would know that God would help him save Israel. The next morning, Gideon found that the fleece was wet with dew and the ground was dry.

But Gideon tested God again. This time, if the fleece was dry and the ground was wet, he would know that God's promise was true. Again, that's exactly what he found in the morning.

At last, Gideon believed and obeyed God.

Art by
AWA
Age 10,
MALI

GIDEON'S ARMY

Judges 7

G ideon was ready to lead Israel's army against the huge Midianite army. Israel's army had thirty-two thousand soldiers. But God told Gideon there were too many men! Israel would brag about how they had won the battle, instead of how God had helped them.

God told Gideon to send home any of the men who were afraid. Ten thousand men remained.

God said there were still too many men. So Gideon took them to the water to drink. Whoever scooped up the water in his hands and lapped it like a dog could stay. The rest had to leave.

Art by
MADISON
Age 10,
UNITED
STATES

Only three hundred men stayed. But God told Gideon they would win the battle.

Gideon split the men into three groups. Each man carried a trumpet and a jar with a torch inside. They surrounded the Midianite army at night. Gideon and his group blew their trumpets and smashed their jars. The other groups did the same.

The Midianite soldiers woke up suddenly, surrounded by noise and firelight. They were terrified. God confused the Midianite soldiers so they fought against each other. Gideon and his army won the battle!

Art by
ASHWEN
Age 12,
SOUTH
AFRICA

SAMSON
and the
PHILISTINES

Judges 13:2–5, 24, 14:5–6, 15:1–16:31

O ne day, an angel appeared to the wife of a man named Manoah. The angel told her that she would have a son. He said that the woman's son must not eat certain foods and he should never cut his hair. The angel also told her that her son would help defeat one of Israel's enemies—the Philistines.

When this son was born, his parents named him Samson. The Spirit of the LORD gave Samson great strength. Samson once killed a lion with his bare hands.

The Philistines sent an army after Samson. He let some Israelites tie him up and hand him over to the Philistines. But as soon as the Philistines came near, Samson easily snapped the ropes. Then he grabbed the jawbone of a donkey and used it as a weapon to kill one thousand men!

Samson fell in love with a woman named Delilah. The Philistines offered to pay Delilah to find out why Samson was so strong. Delilah asked Samson the secret to his strength, but he lied to her. He said that he would become weak if he was tied up with bowstrings that had not been dried. Delilah tied him up and had men ready to attack him. But Samson broke the strings.

Art by
ANNA
Age 10,
GREECE

Delilah asked him again what made him so strong. Samson lied and told her that he would become weak if he was tied with ropes that had never been used. Delilah tied him up and again had men ready to attack. But Samson had tricked her again. He tricked her another time after that.

Finally, when she asked yet again, Samson told her the truth. Because of a promise to God, his hair had never been cut. If anyone cut his hair, Samson would become weak.

When Samson was sleeping, a man shaved off his hair. This time the Philistines were able to tie him up. The LORD had left Samson. They blinded him and took him to prison.

As time passed, Samson's hair began to grow back, and his strength returned. The Philistines had a great feast at their temple. They wanted to make fun of Samson. They led him to the temple and stood him between two pillars. Samson asked God to help him defeat his enemies. He knocked down the pillars and the building crashed to the ground. Samson died with the Philistines in their temple.

Art by
ANNA
Age 10,
GREECE

RUTH
IS
CHOSEN

Book of Ruth

A man from Israel went to Moab to search for food. He took his wife, Naomi, and their two sons. In Moab, the sons married women named Orpah and Ruth.

Some time later, the man and both his sons died. Naomi was alone. She decided to return home to Bethlehem in Israel. She told her sons' wives to stay in Moab, where they had families. Orpah said goodbye, but Ruth refused to leave Naomi.

"Where you go, I will go," Ruth promised. "Your people shall be my people, and your God my God."

Naomi returned to Bethlehem, with Ruth. They were poor and needed food, so Ruth worked hard gathering grain that workers left behind in a field.

The field where Ruth gathered grain belonged to a man named Boaz. He was Naomi's relative. Boaz saw that Ruth was a hard worker. He showed kindness to Ruth by giving her food and water.

Because Boaz was a relative, Naomi wanted him to marry Ruth. Boaz first had to check if another relative would marry her. When that man refused, Boaz married Ruth. Ruth became the great-grandmother of King David.

Art by
ALONDRA
Age 12,
MEXICO

A VOICE in the NIGHT

1 Samuel 1:1–2, 20–28, 3:1–21

Hannah had no children. She prayed for God to give her a son. She promised God that her son would serve him. God answered her prayer, and Hannah named her son Samuel.

When Samuel was a young child, Hannah brought him to the tabernacle. The tabernacle was the place where the people of Israel worshiped God. Samuel lived there and served God.

One night while Samuel was in bed, he heard a voice call out his name.

Samuel went to Eli the priest. "Here I am!" he said. But Eli hadn't called him. He sent Samuel back to bed.

A second time, Samuel heard his name called. Again, Eli sent Samuel back to bed.

Samuel heard the voice a third time! This time, Eli knew that the LORD was calling Samuel.

"Go, lie down," said Eli. "And if he calls you, say, 'Speak, LORD, for your servant hears.'"

God called again, saying "Samuel! Samuel!" This time, Samuel said, "Speak, for your servant hears."

God told Samuel that Eli's sons had been wicked, so he was going to punish Eli's family. At first, Samuel was afraid to tell Eli what God said. But he finally gave Eli God's message, and Eli accepted it.

Samuel grew up and became one of God's prophets.

Art by
MARIA
Age 9,
VENEZUELA

SAUL
Becomes
KING

1 Samuel 8–10

When Samuel was an old man, he made his sons judges in Israel. But his sons were not good judges. They took bribes and were dishonest. The other leaders of Israel complained to Samuel about his sons. They told Samuel that his sons were not good leaders like Samuel had been. They wanted a king to rule over them.

Samuel didn't like what the leaders said. But God told him, "Listen to what the people say. They haven't rejected you—they have rejected me."

So Samuel listened to the people. And God chose a king for them.

A young man named Saul lived in the land of Benjamin. He was the most handsome man in Israel. One day, Saul and a servant went to look for some donkeys that were lost. They couldn't find the donkeys anywhere. The servant said they should go to Samuel. Maybe he could tell them where to look.

As soon as Samuel saw Saul, God told Samuel, "This is the man I've chosen to be your king."

Samuel poured oil on Saul's head as a sign that God had chosen him. Saul would become Israel's first king.

Art by
WALEED
Age 12,
PAKISTAN

A NEW KING for ISRAEL

1 Samuel 16:1–13

The LORD God chose Saul to be Israel's first king. At first, Saul was a good king. But then he began to disobey the LORD. So the LORD chose a new king for Israel.

God sent his prophet Samuel to the town of Bethlehem. There, Samuel met a man named Jesse, who had eight sons. One of them would become Israel's new king.

Samuel thought Jesse's oldest son would surely make a good king. But he was not the one the LORD chose. The LORD told Samuel that what matters most is what is in a person's heart—not how they look on the outside.

Jesse's second son walked by. But he was not the one the LORD chose. Soon, Samuel had seen seven of Jesse's sons. None of them was the king the LORD chose. "Are all your sons here?" Samuel asked.

Art by
DANIEL
Age 9,
UKRAINE

Jesse told Samuel that he had one more son. He was taking care of the sheep.

The last son was David. The LORD told Samuel, "He is the one." Samuel poured oil on David's head. David would be the next king.

DAVID
and
GOLIATH

1 Samuel 17

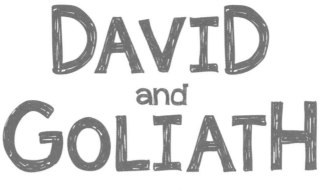

G od had chosen David to be Israel's next king, but David
didn't become king right away. For a while, he stayed
at home with his family and tended the sheep. One day,
David took food to his brothers in the army. They were fighting
against the Philistines, who were enemies of Israel.

At the battlefield, David saw a huge Philistine soldier
named Goliath. He was over nine feet tall! His coat of armor
weighed more than one hundred pounds. Each day,
Goliath shouted at the army of Israel, challenging them
to send out a man to fight him.

All the men in Israel's army were afraid of Goliath.
But David said that he would fight Goliath. When
David tended the sheep, he killed a bear
and a lion. He knew

God had protected him then, and God would protect him in a fight against the Philistine.

King Saul gave David his armor, but it was too big for David to wear. Instead, David went to meet Goliath with only his staff, a sling, and five smooth stones.

Goliath made fun of David. But David said, "I come to you in the name of the LORD, and I will strike you down."

David placed a stone in his sling and swung it around. The stone flew and hit Goliath in the forehead. Goliath fell to the ground, and David ran up and took his sword. When the Philistines saw that Goliath was dead, they ran away.

Art by
JANA
Age 10,
BELARUS

JONATHAN Helps DAVID

1 Samuel 18–20

After David defeated Goliath, he went to live with King Saul. David became best friends with the king's son Jonathan. He married the king's daughter Michal. The people of Israel loved David. They sang about how great he was. Jonathan and Michal loved David. But King Saul did not.

King Saul became so angry that he plotted to kill David. But Michal and Jonathan helped keep David safe.

Once, Michal helped David escape from Saul's men by lowering him out a window. She made it look like David was sleeping in bed. Then she told the men that David couldn't come out. "He is sick," she said. And David escaped to safety.

Another time, Jonathan promised to find out if the king really wanted to hurt David. For two days, David hid from the king. This made Saul so angry that he threw a spear at Jonathan! Jonathan was not hurt, but now he knew the truth. His father wanted to kill David.

Jonathan and David came up with a secret way to warn David if he was in danger. Jonathan went to the field where David was hiding, and he practiced shooting some arrows. Then Jonathan said to a young boy, "Isn't the arrow beyond you?" That was their secret code. It meant the king still wanted to hurt David, and he should run away and not return.

David heard the message and knew that he had to leave. He sadly said goodbye to his best friend, Jonathan.

Art by
SHILO OBED
Age 9,
MALAYSIA

89

DAVID RUNS from SAUL

1 Samuel 24, 26

David ran away and hid from King Saul. But King Saul still wanted to kill him. He took three thousand men with him to look for David.

During the search, Saul went into a cave. He didn't know that David and his men were hiding in it. David could have easily sneaked up on Saul and killed him. But he refused to harm Saul, because God had chosen Saul as king. David secretly cut off part of Saul's robe, and told his men not to hurt Saul.

After Saul left the cave, David called out to him. He told Saul that he could have killed him but chose not to. He held up the piece of Saul's robe.

Saul cried. He said, "You are a better man than I am. You have been good to me but I did bad things to you. I know that you will surely be king."

Soon, however, Saul was back to chasing David.

One night, David and
Abishai, one of David's men, sneaked
into Saul's camp. Saul was asleep with a spear next
to him. Abishai wanted to kill Saul with the spear, but David
wouldn't allow it. Instead, he took Saul's spear and water jug and
went to a hill. He shouted out to Saul and showed him the spear.

Once again, David could have killed Saul, but he didn't.

ABIGAIL
Helps
DAVID

1 Samuel 25

N abal was a very rich man. He had a large flock of sheep and goats. He had a wise and beautiful wife named Abigail. But Nabal was selfish and behaved badly.

One day, David sent ten messengers to Nabal.

David's men greeted Nabal. "Peace be with you," they said. They explained to him that they had been living in the wilderness. They had guarded Nabal's shepherds and flocks. But they had never taken any of Nabal's animals. Then they asked Nabal to share his food with them.

Nabal refused to give food or water to David and his men. This answer made David angry. He took four hundred men to attack Nabal.

Art by
SINDY
Age 9,
SINGAPORE

Abigail found out that her husband wouldn't share with David and his men. She quickly loaded bread, meat, and other food on donkeys and went to meet David. When she saw him, she begged him not to kill anyone. David thanked God for sending Abigail to stop him from harming Nabal.

Ten days later, Nabal died.

Art by
ANTHONY
Age 12,
MADAGASCAR

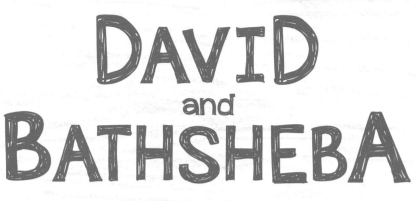

DAVID and BATHSHEBA

2 Samuel 11–12

After the death of Saul, David became king. David sent his army off to fight a war, while he stayed at home. One day, he noticed a beautiful woman named Bathsheba. David wanted Bathsheba to be his wife. But she was already married to Uriah, a man in David's army.

David came up with a terrible plan. He ordered Uriah to the front of a battle, where he was killed. Now David could marry Bathsheba.

God knew that David had done wrong. So God sent a prophet named Nathan to see David. Nathan told David a story about a poor man who had a lamb that he loved. A rich man took the poor man's lamb to feed his guest.

David grew angry, saying, "The man who has done this deserves to die."

But Nathan replied, "You are the man!"
Nathan reminded David that God had made him
king and rescued him from Saul. Yet David had
done an evil thing.

David was sorry for what he had done. God forgave
David. But David had family troubles for the rest
of his life.

SOLOMON the WISE KING

1 Kings 3–8

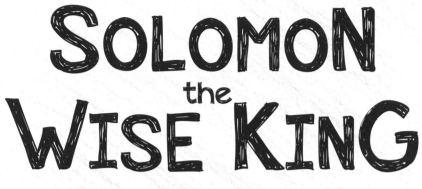

King David and Bathsheba had a son named Solomon. When David died, Solomon became the king of Israel.

One night, God appeared to Solomon in a dream. In the dream, God told Solomon to ask him for anything he wanted.

Solomon asked for wisdom to understand what is right so he could be a good king. Solomon's answer made God happy. He gave Solomon the wisdom he had asked for. God also gave him riches and a good reputation.

Later, Solomon announced that he would build a house for the LORD. He gathered all the supplies he would need. And in Solomon's fourth year as king of Israel, his workers began building the temple.

Art by
VUYO
Age 11,
MALAWI

The temple was a huge building! It was 90 feet long, 30 feet wide, and 45 feet high. The walls were lined with cedar wood. It had beautiful furniture made of gold and bronze.

After seven years of hard work, the temple was finished. Solomon gathered the people of Israel to dedicate it to God. God's glory appeared as a cloud and filled the beautiful new temple.

The QUEEN OF SHEBA Visits SOLOMON

1 Kings 10:1–13

God gave King Solomon great wisdom. People in other lands began to hear about him. One day, the queen of the land of Sheba visited King Solomon. She wanted to find out if the stories about his wisdom were true. So she asked Solomon questions to test him.

Solomon answered all her hard questions. Then he showed the queen his servants and his beautiful palace. She also saw the many offerings Solomon gave at the temple.

Before visiting Solomon, the queen didn't believe what she heard about him. But now that she had seen him with her own eyes, she said, "Your wisdom and prosperity are even greater than I had heard." The queen praised the LORD God for making Solomon king.

The queen of Sheba had brought with her many camels carrying gold, spices, and jewels. She gave these as gifts to King Solomon. In return, Solomon also gave many gifts to the queen before she returned home.

Art by
POLINA
Age 9,
SOUTH
AFRICA

ELIJAH
and the
WIDOW
of Zarephath

1 Kings 16:29–17:24

Years after King Solomon died, the wicked Ahab became king of Israel. Ahab and his wife, Queen Jezebel, led the people of Israel to worship a god called Baal. This made the LORD, the God of Israel, angry. The prophet Elijah warned Ahab that it would not rain for three years.

Without rain, plants couldn't grow. Food began to run out. God sent Elijah to see a widow in the town of Zarephath. She would give him food.

When Elijah arrived at Zarephath, he saw a widow gathering sticks. He asked her for water and bread. But the widow told him she only had a little bit of flour and oil left. She planned to make one last meal to eat with her son, and then they both would die.

Elijah had a message from God for the woman. He told her that the flour and oil would not run out until the rain came again.

Elijah stayed with the widow and her son. The flour and oil never ran out during the time there was no rain. They all had enough bread to eat.

Later, the widow's son got sick and died. Elijah asked God to let the child live again. God heard Elijah's prayer. The boy returned to life!

Art by
MARIA
Age 12,
PORTUGAL

CONTEST on MOUNT CARMEL

1 Kings 18

F or three years, God did not send rain on Israel. The people had very little food. Even King Ahab had trouble finding grass and water for his animals.

God sent his prophet Elijah to speak to King Ahab. "I didn't cause Israel's troubles. You did," Elijah announced. "You abandoned the commandments and you followed the Baals."

Elijah challenged King Ahab to a contest. King Ahab, the people of Israel, and four hundred-fifty prophets of Baal would meet Elijah on Mount Carmel. The prophets of Baal would offer a bull as a sacrifice to Baal. Elijah would offer a bull to God. They would both have wood for their offerings, but no fire. The prophets would call on Baal.

Elijah would call on God. The god who answered by sending the fire was the real God.

The prophets of Baal went first. They called to Baal all morning. "O Baal, answer us!" they cried. They danced around, but no fire came.

Elijah made fun of them and said, "Maybe he is asleep and must be awakened."

They kept shouting, but Baal never answered.

Next it was Elijah's turn. He placed wood on the altar and put his offering on the wood. Then he asked for four jugs of water. Three times, the jugs were filled and water was poured on the bull and the wood.

"O LORD, God of Abraham, Isaac, and Israel," Elijah prayed. "Show us today that you are God in Israel." Elijah asked God to answer him and to turn the people's hearts back to God.

Art by
EMY
Age 10,
DOMINICAN
REPUBLIC

God answered Elijah! Fire fell from the sky. It burned the offering, the wood, and the water. The people bowed to the ground and cried out, "The LORD is God."

The prophets of Baal were captured and killed.

Then Elijah told his servant to look toward the sea. What did he see? The servant didn't see anything. Seven times Elijah sent his servant to look at the sea. Finally, the servant saw a small cloud. Rain was coming!

The power of God came on Elijah. He ran ahead, faster than King Ahab's chariot!

Art by
DAISY
Age 12,
DOMINICAN
REPUBLIC

105

ELIJAH
Goes to
HEAVEN

2 Kings 2:1–14

E lijah served God for many years. He knew that soon the time would come for him to leave. The man who would take his place as prophet had already been chosen. His name was Elisha.

Other prophets asked Elisha, "Do you know that today the LORD will take away your master?" But Elisha already knew this. He traveled with Elijah and didn't want to leave his side.

When they got to the Jordan River, Elijah rolled up his cloak and hit the river with it. The water split apart, and the two walked across on the dry ground.

Elijah asked Elisha if there was anything he could do for Elisha before he had to leave.

Elisha answered, "Please let there be a double portion of your spirit on me."

Elijah explained that Elisha had asked for a hard thing. But Elisha would receive what he had asked if he saw Elijah leave the earth.

As they walked, chariots of fire and horses of fire appeared. Elijah was taken away to heaven in a whirlwind. His cloak fell from him.

Elisha watched as Elijah was taken away. He picked up the cloak and hit the water of the Jordan River. The water split apart.

Art by **STEFANIA** Age 11, RUSSIA

ELISHA
and the
WIDOW'S OIL

2 Kings 4:1–7

One day, a woman came to the prophet Elisha for help. Her husband had been one of the sons of the prophets of God. Now he was dead, and the widow could not pay her bills. If she didn't pay, someone might take her two sons away as slaves.

Elisha asked the widow what she had in her house. All she had was a jar of oil. Elisha told her to borrow as many empty jars from her neighbors as she could and then pour the oil from her one jar into all the jars.

The woman did as she was told. As she poured oil in the jars, the oil kept flowing! She filled up all the jars.

She called for one of her sons to bring more jars.

"There are no more," he said.

The oil stopped flowing.

"Go, sell the oil and pay your debts," Elisha told her.

Again, the woman did what Elisha said. She paid her bills and had enough money left over to take care of her sons.

Art by
TATEVIK
Age 10,
ARMENIA

ELISHA
and the
WOMAN
of Shunem

2 Kings 4:8–37

A s a prophet of God, Elisha traveled all over. When he went to the town of Shunem, a rich woman invited him to eat at her house. Later, the woman asked her husband to build a small room for Elisha in their home. This way, Elisha would have a place to sleep whenever he traveled to Shunem.

Elisha wanted to do something nice for the woman since she had showed such kindness to him.

Gehazi, Elisha's servant, thought of something he could do for her. The woman and her husband didn't have a son. Elisha told the woman that in a year, she would have a son. Elisha's words came true! The woman and her husband were very happy.

Years later, their son died. The woman went to Elisha for help.

Elisha gave his staff to Gehazi and told him to lay it on the boy's face. Gehazi did just what Elisha said. But the boy was still dead.

Art by
HAFSA
Age 11,
PAKISTAN

So Elisha went to the woman's house. Sure
enough, the boy was lying dead on the bed. Elisha
prayed to God. The boy sneezed seven times and opened his
eyes. He was alive!

NAAMAN'S LEPROSY

2 Kings 5

Naaman was the leader of the army in a country called Syria. His army had won victory after victory, but Naaman had a problem. He had a terrible skin disease called leprosy.

Naaman's servant said that she wished Naaman could go see the prophet in Israel. She was talking about Elisha.

"He would cure him of his leprosy," the servant said.

The king of Syria gave Naaman permission to go to Israel. Naaman took with him gifts of silver, gold, and clothes to give to the king of Israel. But the king couldn't cure Naaman.

"Let him come to me," Elisha the prophet said.

Naaman went to Elisha's house, but Elisha didn't come out. Instead, he sent a messenger to tell Naaman to wash himself seven times in the Jordan River. This made Naaman angry. Wash in the Jordan River? He thought the rivers in his own country were much better.

Art by
FRANCESCO
Age 10,
ITALY

Naaman's servants convinced him to do what
Elisha said. Naaman washed in the Jordan River seven
times. He came out of the water cured!

"Now I know there is no God in all the earth but in Israel,"
Naaman said.

The HIDDEN KING

2 Kings 11

The nation of Israel split into two kingdoms: Israel in the north and Judah in the south. The king of Judah was killed. Now who would rule Judah? Athaliah, the king's mother, wanted to rule. But she had to make sure none of the king's sons would stand in her way. So she had the royal princes killed.

Athaliah didn't know that one prince had escaped. Baby Joash had been snatched away from the other princes and hidden in the temple.

While Athaliah ruled over Judah, a priest protected baby Joash. He had guards watch over the palace and the temple. The guards did what he asked.

Six years later, the priest brought Joash out of hiding. He placed a crown on Joash's head and anointed him as king. Joash was only seven years old!

The people cried out, "Long live the king!"

Athaliah heard the shouting and saw Joash with the crown. She tore her clothes and called out, "Treason! Treason!" The people had turned against her. They replaced her with Joash, and the priest ordered that she be put to death.

HEZEKIAH'S ILLNESS

2 Kings 20:1–11

Many years after Israel split into two kingdoms, Hezekiah became king of Judah. He was a good king and followed God's laws.

One day Hezekiah became sick. The prophet Isaiah warned him that he would die. Hezekiah cried and prayed to God. He reminded God how faithfully he had served him.

God gave Isaiah a message for Hezekiah. God had heard the king's prayer and would heal him. Hezekiah would live fifteen more years!

Isaiah gave the king God's message. Then he said to put a mixture made of figs on Hezekiah's skin so it would heal. But

Hezekiah wanted to know what sign he would see that God would heal him.

Isaiah asked Hezekiah if he wanted to see the sun's shadow move forward ten steps or backward ten steps. Hezekiah said he wanted to see the shadow move backward. So Isaiah called to God, and the shadow moved backward ten steps. This was God's sign that he would heal Hezekiah.

JOSIAH
and the
BOOK OF THE LAW

2 Kings 22

Josiah became king of Judah when he was only eight years old. His father had done wrong things that displeased God. But Josiah did what was right.

King Josiah knew the temple needed repairs. He told a priest to count the money people had given. This money would be used to pay workers and buy supplies.

The same priest who counted the money made a discovery in the temple. He found a copy of the Book of the Law. The people had forgotten about it.

The king listened to the laws that were in the book. He was upset to learn that his people had not been obeying

God. He sent men to Huldah, a prophet, to ask what should be done.

God gave Huldah a message to tell the people that they had done wrong. The people had forgotten to follow God's ways. This made God angry, and he would send disaster upon the people.

King Josiah was sorry. For the rest of his life, he helped the people obey God. God made sure Josiah didn't face the hard times. God waited until after Josiah died to allow the bad things to happen.

Art by
THADEUS
Age 11,
PHILIPPINES

119

The
PROPHET
in the
WELL

Jeremiah 37–38

J eremiah was chosen as a prophet at a young age. He spoke God's messages. But many people didn't want to hear what he had to say.

Jeremiah had bad news for the people of Jerusalem. Trouble was coming, as God had promised. The army of Babylon would defeat Judah.

King Zedekiah of Judah asked the Egyptian army for help. The Egyptians chased away the army of Babylon. But Jeremiah told them

help get me OUT OF here!

the Egyptians would soon leave. Then the army from Babylon would return.

The king's officers didn't like what Jeremiah said. They put him in prison, but Jeremiah continued to speak God's messages. He told the people to surrender to the Babylonians. The king's officers wanted to kill Jeremiah. They threw him into a muddy well instead.

One of the king's men saw how badly Jeremiah had been treated. He told the king that Jeremiah would die of hunger. King

Zedekiah had Jeremiah pulled out of the well. Jeremiah remained a prisoner until his words came true. The army from Babylon returned.

Art by
SOPHIE
Age 9,
UNITED
KINGDOM

A CITY DESTROYED

2 Kings 25:1–21

After King Josiah died, God sent disaster on the land of
Judah. King Nebuchadnezzar of Babylon came with his
army. They surrounded the city of Jerusalem for almost
two years. No one could get in or out. The food ran out. The
people in the city began to starve.

One night, all the soldiers of Judah tried to escape from
the city. But King Nebuchadnezzar's army stopped them. They
captured Judah's king, Zedekiah, and blinded him. They took
King Zedekiah to Babylon in chains.

King Nebuchadnezzar's army destroyed the city of Jerusalem.
They burned the temple King Solomon had built. They stole the
beautiful gold and silver items from the temple. The army burned
the houses and other buildings. Then they broke down the walls
around Jerusalem.

The city was destroyed.

And many people in Judah were taken to Babylon as captives.

REBUILDING
the Wall of
JERUSALEM

Nehemiah 1–6

Many people in Judah were taken away to Babylon. But God spoke to them through prophets like Isaiah and Jeremiah. God promised they would go home someday. That promise came true. People began to return to Jerusalem. But the wall around Jerusalem had been torn down. People living there were not safe from enemies.

Nehemiah was an Israelite. He worked for the king of Persia. When Nehemiah heard about the broken wall, he cried. He prayed for the people in Jerusalem. Then he asked the king for permission to go to Jerusalem to rebuild the wall.

124

In Jerusalem, Nehemiah inspected the wall. Then he organized the people to rebuild it. This was dangerous work. Enemies could attack the workers at any moment. The builders worked with a building tool in one hand and a weapon in the other.

Several men tried to harm Nehemiah. But Nehemiah and the others kept working on the wall.

After fifty-two days of hard work, the wall was finished.

Art by
HANNA
Age 10,
BOLIVIA

ESTHER'S CHALLENGE

Book of Esther

The king of Persia threw a huge party. He told his wife to come so everyone could see how pretty she was, but she refused. The king was angry. He decided to get a new wife.

The king ordered all the beautiful young women in the kingdom to come to him. Esther was one of them. She was Jewish. Her family had been taken from their homeland of Israel. Her mother and father had died, so she had been raised by her cousin Mordecai.

When the king met Esther, he chose her as queen.

Mordecai told Esther not to tell anyone that she was a Jew. She also didn't tell anyone that Mordecai was her relative.

Now, the people in Persia knew that Mordecai was a Jew. One day, the king's top official, Haman, passed by the gate where Mordecai was standing. Everyone else bowed down to Haman. Mordecai refused to bow, which made Haman very angry. He came up with a plan to have all the Jews in Persia put to death.

Haman asked the king for permission to carry out his plan. The king wrote a law allowing Haman to have the Jews killed. Once a law was made, it could not be changed.

Mordecai told this terrible news to Esther. He said she must ask the king to stop Haman's plan! If Esther went to the king without being invited, she could be put to death. But if the king held out his scepter, then Esther could approach him.

Art by
CARLOS
Age 10,
NICARAGUA

Mordecai told Esther that perhaps she was born to save the people of Israel.

Esther had an important and dangerous job to do. She told Mordecai and the Jews to fast for three days. She fasted also. At the end of three days, Esther went to the king. He held out his scepter! Esther was allowed to approach the king. She invited the king and Haman to dinner.

During the meal, Esther told the king about Haman's evil plan to kill the Jews. Then it was time to tell the king her secret.

Esther told the king that she was a Jew.
She begged him to save her and her people.
The king was so upset that he put Haman to death. He couldn't
undo Haman's law, but he made a new law. It said that the Jews
could defend themselves from anyone who tried to
harm them.

The people celebrated because their lives were
saved. This celebration was the start of a new
holiday called Purim.

Art by
MARIANA
Age 10,
PORTUGAL

JOB SUFFERS

Book of Job

Job lived a long time ago in the land of Uz. He had ten children, big flocks of animals, and many servants. Job was a good man who worshiped God. One day, Satan appeared before God. God asked, "Have you noticed my servant Job? He is an honest man who honors God and turns away from evil."

Satan said that Job worshiped God because God had made him rich. "But take away all that you have given him," Satan said, "and he will curse you."

God allowed Satan to take everything from Job. One by one, Job's servants brought him the bad news. Enemies had killed his servants, said the one servant who escaped. Fire from heaven had burned up Job's sheep and servants, said another. Another messenger told Job his camels had been stolen. A great wind blew down Job's son's house and killed all his children, said a third. Job lost everything. He even lost his health, as painful sores covered his body.

Job's wife wanted him to curse God. Job's friends thought he must have made God angry. But that wasn't true. God told Job that he is in charge of everything because he created everything.

Job did not curse God. He praised God. He trusted that God was in charge. Job had proven Satan wrong.

Later, God healed Job. And he gave Job ten more children and twice as many riches as he had before.

Art by
COLLINS
Age 12,
NIGERIA

A
SPECIAL
DIET

Daniel 1

King Nebuchadnezzar of Babylon took many Israelites as slaves. The king chose some of the finest young men to serve in his palace. The young men had to be handsome and smart. Daniel and three of his friends were chosen.

Daniel and his friends were faithful to God. They didn't want to eat the king's rich food or drink his wine. It would go against God's laws. So Daniel asked if they could eat only vegetables and drink only water.

The officer in charge didn't like this idea. He was afraid Daniel and his friends would become sick. But Daniel asked if they could test his idea for ten days. Then, the officer could compare Daniel and his friends to the young men who ate the king's food.

The officer agreed to let Daniel and his friends try the special diet. After ten days, they looked

132

Art by
DENIS
Age 12,
MOLDOVA

healthier than the other young men. From then on, they only ate the foods God wanted them to eat.

The FIERY FURNACE

Daniel 3

K ing Nebuchadnezzar did not worship the God of Israel. Instead, he had a large golden statue built as a god. He commanded everyone in his kingdom to bow down and worship the statue whenever they heard music playing. If they didn't obey, they would be thrown into a fiery furnace.

Shadrach, Meshach, and Abednego believed in the God of Israel. They refused to worship the statue. When the king found out, he called Shadrach, Meshach, and Abednego before him. He gave them another chance to worship the statue.

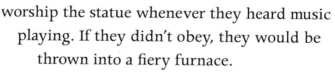

But Shadrach, Meshach, and Abednego said that the God they worshiped could rescue them from the furnace. They also said that even if God did not rescue them, they would not bow down to the golden statue.

This made the king very angry. He ordered that the furnace be made seven times hotter than usual. It was so hot that the men who pushed Shadrach, Meshach, and Abednego into the furnace died!

The king looked into the furnace. The three men were walking around in the fire! A fourth man was with them, shining brightly.

Shadrach, Meshach, and Abednego did not die in the furnace. When they came out, they didn't even smell like smoke! God had saved them. The king praised God.

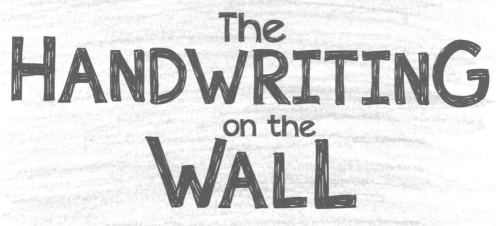

The HANDWRITING on the WALL

Daniel 5

After King Nebuchadnezzar died, Belshazzar became king of Babylon. One night, he threw a huge party. King Belshazzar brought out the gold and silver cups that had been stolen from God's temple. He and his guests drank wine from the cups and praised their gods.

Suddenly a hand appeared out of nowhere! It wrote on a nearby wall. The hand wrote strange words: *mene, mene, tekel, parsin.* The king was scared. He called for his wise men, but they didn't understand the words. Belshazzar promised to reward anyone who told him what the words meant. But no one could do it.

The queen told the king to send for Daniel. She knew Daniel was very wise.

Daniel told the king what the words meant. *Mene* meant that God had numbered the days of Belshazzar's rule. It was about to end. *Tekel* meant the king had been measured and was unworthy of ruling. *Parsin* meant God would give Belshazzar's kingdom to the king's enemies.

That night, the message came true. The king was put to death. A new king named Darius took his place.

Art by
ALONDRA
Age 12,
MEXICO

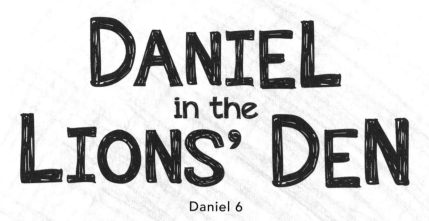

DANIEL in the LIONS' DEN

Daniel 6

King Darius had many officials serving him. Daniel was one of them, and he was better than all the others. The other officials were jealous of Daniel and wanted to get him in trouble with the king. They knew that Daniel prayed to the God of Israel. They asked the king to make a new law. For thirty days, the people could only pray to King Darius. Anyone who broke the law by praying to another god would be thrown into a den filled with hungry lions.

The king agreed and made the law.

Daniel knew about the law, but he continued to pray to God. The other leaders told the king that Daniel had broken the law. The king liked Daniel. He was sad that he had to punish Daniel, but a law said he had to do so.

"May your God save you!" he called as Daniel was thrown into the den of lions. All night long, the king couldn't sleep.

In the morning, he went to the lions' den.

"Daniel, has your God saved you?" the king called out.

Daniel answered, "My God sent his angel and shut the lions' mouths." Daniel was unharmed!

Daniel was brought out of the lions' den. And the men who had complained about him were thrown into the den of lions, along with their families.

Art by
RAJAN
Age 11,
INDIA

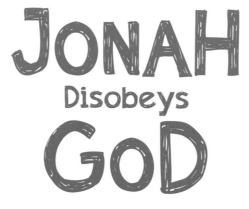

JONAH
Disobeys
GOD

Book of Jonah

God looked on the city of Nineveh and saw the evil things the people were doing. He told his prophet Jonah to go to Nineveh and preach against the city.

Jonah heard God, but he didn't obey. Instead, he got on a ship headed in the opposite direction.

God made a bad storm strike the ship. The sailors were afraid. They wanted to know who caused the storm. They cast lots to find out whose fault it was. When the lot indicated it was Jonah's fault, they questioned him.

Jonah admitted that he was a prophet who had run away from God. He told the sailors to toss him into the sea. As soon as they did, the sea grew calm. But Jonah didn't drown. Instead, he was swallowed by a huge fish.

For three days and nights, Jonah stayed alive in the fish. He prayed to God and thanked God for saving him. God heard Jonah and caused the fish to spit him out on dry land.

This time, Jonah obeyed God. He went to Nineveh and told the people that God would destroy the city in forty days. The people listened to Jonah's message from God and were sorry for the wrongs they had done. They went without food and put on clothes called sackcloth to show they were sorry.

God saw that the people were sorry. He decided not to destroy the city.

This made Jonah angry. He didn't want God to show mercy to the people.

God asked Jonah if it was right for him to be angry.

Jonah went outside the city to see what would happen to the people of Nineveh. God caused a big plant to grow and provide shade for Jonah. But when dawn came the next day, God sent a worm to eat the plant. This made Jonah mad again!

God cared about the people of Nineveh. He said to Jonah, "You pity the plant, which you didn't plant or make grow. Should I not pity Nineveh?"

Art by
SOFIA
Age 9,
ARGENTINA

NEW TESTAMENT

Art by
LEISY
Age 11,
COLOMBIA

A SPECIAL SON

Luke 1:5–25, 57–80

Zechariah was a priest from a town in Judah. He and his wife were good people who loved God. But God had not given them a child.

One day, an angel named Gabriel appeared to Zechariah while he was working in the temple in Jerusalem. "Your prayer has been heard," said Gabriel. "Your wife Elizabeth will have a son, and you will name him John."

The angel explained that the child would grow up to be a prophet. He would be filled with the Spirit of God and would help bring many people of Israel back to God.

"How can I know this is true?" asked Zechariah. Both Zechariah and his wife were old. He didn't understand how they could have children at their age.

The angel told Zechariah that because he did not believe the message, he wouldn't be able to speak until their son was born.

Everything happened just as the angel said. Zechariah left the temple and he couldn't say a word! Later, Elizabeth had a son.

Zechariah's relatives were surprised that the baby was called John. No one in their family was named John. But Zechariah wrote, "His name is John." Suddenly, he was able to speak.

Art by
BRITNEY
Age 11,
MALAYSIA

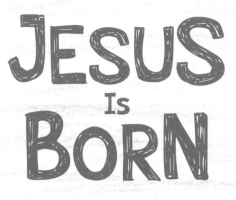

JESUS
Is
BORN

Luke 1:1–4, 26–56, 2:1–21

I n the town of Nazareth, there lived a young woman named Mary. She was engaged to marry Joseph. One day, the angel Gabriel visited Mary.

"Greetings, O favored one," said the angel.

Mary wasn't sure what Gabriel meant by that greeting. But Gabriel had amazing news for Mary—she was going to have a son!

"You will call him Jesus," said Gabriel. "He will be great and will be called the Son of the Most High."

"How can this be?" asked Mary, who was not yet married.

Gabriel said the child would be born through the power of the Most High.

Mary accepted Gabriel's news.

Art by
VENUS
Age 11,
PHILIPPINES

149

At that time, the Roman ruler wanted to know how many people there were in all the lands he ruled. Everyone had to go to their hometown to be counted. So Joseph and Mary traveled to Bethlehem, Joseph's hometown.

When they arrived, it was time for the baby to be born. But the town was crowded and there were no rooms available for Mary and Joseph. In a place where animals were kept, Mary gave birth to a son. She wrapped him in cloths and placed him in a manger.

That night, one of God's angels appeared to a group of shepherds.

"Fear not," the angel said. "I bring you good news. For unto you is born this day in the city of David a Savior." The angel told the shepherds that they would find the baby in a manger.

Suddenly a multitude of angels filled the sky. "Glory to God in the highest" they said. The angels spoke of peace on earth.

The shepherds went to Bethlehem and found the baby, just like the angel said. The shepherds told others what they saw. Mary and Joseph named the baby Jesus.

Art by
VENUS
Age 11,
PHILIPPINES

The WISE MEN

Matthew 2

A group of wise men from the east traveled to Jerusalem. They had seen a star and had followed it.

When they arrived in Jerusalem they asked, "Where is he who has been born king of the Jews?" They wanted to worship this new king.

Their question upset King Herod and the people of Jerusalem. Herod asked the temple leaders what they knew. They told him that long ago a prophet proclaimed that a ruler would be born in the town of Bethlehem. Herod told the wise men to go to Bethlehem and bring news about the child back to him.

The star led the wise men to a place in Bethlehem. There, they found Mary and a young child—Jesus. The wise men worshiped the child and gave him gifts of gold, frankincense, and myrrh. When it was time to leave, the wise men were warned in a dream not to return to King Herod in Jerusalem.

Joseph also had a dream. God's angel told him to run away with Mary and Jesus into Egypt. They got out of Bethlehem in time. Herod sent soldiers to Bethlehem to kill all the boys two years old and under. But Jesus was safe in Egypt.

Art by
ROSSELLA
Age 11,
ITALY

SIMEON AND ANNA SEE JESUS

Luke 2:22–40

The law of Moses said firstborn sons had to be presented to God. Since Jesus was a firstborn son, Mary and Joseph brought him to the temple to present him to the Lord. They gave an offering for their son.

A man named Simeon came to the temple that day. He was a good man who followed God's laws. The Holy Spirit had told Simeon that he would live to see God's promised Messiah.

Simeon saw Jesus with Mary and Joseph. Then he knew God's promise had come true. He picked up the child and praised God. Then he blessed Mary and Joseph, who were amazed at what they had heard.

A widow named Anna was also at the temple. She was a prophet who spoke God's messages. Like Simeon, she thanked God for the child.

Art by
MOSTEENA
Age 11,
MALAWI

Mary and Joseph returned home to Nazareth with Jesus. There, he grew to become a wise young man, favored by God.

A
SON LOST
and
FOUND

Luke 2:41–52

It was time for the Passover, the yearly feast that celebrates God's rescue of the Israelites from Egypt. Jesus was twelve years old. He went with his family to Jerusalem to celebrate the Passover.

When the feast ended, Jesus's family started for home. After a whole day of traveling, Mary and Joseph realized they hadn't seen Jesus. They thought he was with the others in their group. But none of their relatives or friends had seen Jesus either.

Mary and Joseph made the trip back to Jerusalem. Three days passed before they found Jesus. He was in the temple, listening to the teachers and asking questions. Everyone who heard Jesus was amazed by his wisdom.

"Why did you do this to us?" Mary asked Jesus. Mary and Joseph had been very worried as they searched for Jesus.

"Why were you looking for me? Didn't you know that I must be in my Father's house?" Jesus asked.

Jesus returned home with his parents to Nazareth in Galilee. He continued to grow in wisdom. God and people were pleased with Jesus.

Art by
LUKSHAN
Age 12,
SRI LANKA

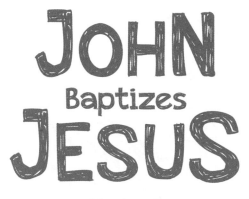

JOHN Baptizes JESUS

Matthew 3

Zechariah and Elizabeth's son, John, grew up to become a prophet. John preached in the desert, warning the people to obey God and stop doing wrong things. He ate locusts and wild honey, and he wore clothes made from camel's hair.

He was called John the Baptist because he baptized people in the Jordan River. The people who came to be baptized admitted that they had done wrong things. They wanted to change and follow God's laws.

One day, a man came to John to be baptized. It was Jesus. He was about thirty years old at the time.

At first, John said to Jesus, "I need to be baptized by you."

But John agreed to baptize Jesus. After Jesus came up out of the water, the heavens opened. The Spirit of God landed on Jesus like a dove. A voice spoke to him saying, "This is my beloved Son, with whom I am well pleased."

159

JESUS Is TEMPTED

Matthew 4:1–11

After Jesus was baptized, the Spirit of God led him to the wilderness. He stayed there forty days and nights without food.

Along came Satan—who is also called the devil—to tempt Jesus to do something wrong. "If you are the Son of God, command these stones to become loaves of bread," Satan said.

Jesus was hungry, but he didn't do what Satan told him to do. Jesus replied, "It is written in Scriptures that man shall not live by bread alone, but by every word that comes from the mouth of God."

But Satan was not finished. He took Jesus to the top of the temple in Jerusalem. "If you are the Son of God," Satan said, "throw yourself down from here." Satan told Jesus that God would send his angels to take care of him.

Again, Jesus stood strong against the Devil.

He quoted another verse from Scriptures, saying, "You shall not put the Lord your God to the test."

On a mountaintop, the Devil showed Jesus kingdoms around the world. He promised to give them to Jesus if Jesus worshiped him.

But Jesus said, "Be gone, Satan! For it is written, 'You shall worship the Lord your God and him only shall you serve.'"

Finally, Satan left him alone. Angels came to take care of Jesus.

Art by
COLLINS
Age 12,
NIGERIA

JESUS'S First DISCIPLES

Luke 5:1–11, 27–32

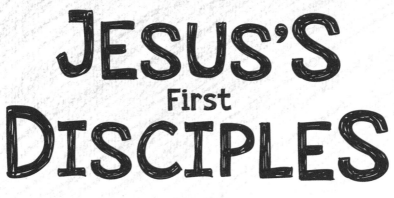

Jesus traveled around teaching people about God. One day, a crowd gathered at the Sea of Galilee to hear him speak. Jesus stepped onto a boat owned by a fisherman named Simon. Jesus taught the people from Simon's boat.

When he finished teaching, Jesus told Simon to take the boat out into the water and use his nets to catch fish. Simon had fished all night without catching any fish. But he listened to Jesus, and he let down the nets. Soon, the nets were full of fish. They were so heavy that Simon called his friends James and John over to help him.

After looking at all the fish, Simon fell down in front of Jesus in amazement.

Simon, James, and John left their fishing
jobs and everything else to become Jesus's disciples.

Jesus would teach them, and they would follow his
example. Jesus gave Simon a new name—Peter.

Peter, James, and John were not the only ones Jesus chose
as disciples. Later Jesus saw a tax collector named Levi and told
him, "Follow me." Levi left everything and followed Jesus. Soon,
Jesus had twelve disciples.

Art by
RINAT
Age 9,
UKRAINE

JESUS'S
First
MIRACLE

John 2

Jesus was invited to a wedding, along with his disciples and his mother, Mary. The wedding was in Cana, a small town close to Nazareth.

At the wedding feast, the guests ate and drank. Soon, they ran out of wine. Mary told Jesus what had happened.

"What does this have to do with me?" Jesus asked. "My time has not yet come."

But Mary told the servants, "Do whatever he tells you."

Jesus told the servants to fill six huge jars with water. Each jar held about twenty or thirty gallons of water. Once the jars were filled with water, Jesus told the servants to give some of it to the master of the feast. The master was in charge of the food and wine.

The master of the wedding feast tasted what the servants brought. The water had been turned into wine! He said to the groom, "You have kept the good wine until now."

Jesus had performed his first miracle.

Art by
EUGENIA
Age 12,
RUSSIA

165

HELPING a FRIEND

Mark 2:1–12

One day, a large crowd gathered to hear Jesus teach in a house. Some men wanted Jesus to help their friend. Their friend could not walk, so they carried him on a mat to see Jesus. When the men got to the house where Jesus was teaching, it was so crowded they couldn't get in the door.

There was only one way to get their friend to Jesus. The men climbed up to the roof and made a hole in it. Then they lowered their friend into the room.

Jesus saw the men and their friend who couldn't walk. He saw they had faith. He told the man on the mat, "Your sins are forgiven."

Some of the teachers of the law of Moses were sitting there. They didn't like what Jesus said. They believed that only God could forgive people for the bad things they did!

Jesus knew what they were thinking. He asked, "Which is easier, to say—'Your sins are forgiven,' or, 'Rise, take up your bed and walk'?" To prove that he had the authority on earth to do both, Jesus told the man on the mat, "Pick up your bed and go home."

The man stood and walked! Everyone was amazed.

Art by
NICOLAS
Age 9,
VENEZUELA

The SERMON on the MOUNT

Matthew 5–7

One day, the disciples and a large crowd of people followed Jesus to a mountainside. There, Jesus taught them many things about how to please God. He began with a list of blessings. He told them:

"Blessed are the poor in spirit, for theirs is the kingdom of heaven."

"Blessed are those who mourn," he said, "for they shall be comforted."

"Blessed are the merciful, for they shall receive mercy."

Jesus continued, "Blessed are the pure in heart, for they shall see God."

Next, Jesus taught the people to love and forgive their enemies instead of hating them.

He also reminded them not to worry about things like clothes or food. Jesus told the people that just like God takes care of the birds, he will take care of them.

Art by
ABANOUB
Age 12,
EGYPT

Jesus taught that it is wrong to judge other people. He said that each person should be concerned with the wrong things they do rather than the wrong things other people do.

And he said that each person should treat others just like they want to be treated. He said, "Whatever you wish that others would do to you, do also to them."

Jesus's words amazed everyone who heard him.

The LORD'S PRAYER

Matthew 6:5–15

One day, Jesus taught his disciples how to talk to God. He didn't want them to pray in public, hoping to impress others. Instead, Jesus told his followers to talk to God privately, where only God would see and hear them.

Jesus gave them an example of how to pray to God. He said this prayer:

"Our Father in heaven,
 hallowed be your name.
 Your kingdom come,
 your will be done,
 on earth as it is in heaven.

Give us this day our daily bread,
and forgive us our debts,
as we also have forgiven our debtors.
And lead us not into temptation,
but deliver us from evil."

Jesus reminded his followers that if they
refused to forgive others,
then God would not
forgive them.

Art by
DANIELA
Age 12,
MEXICO

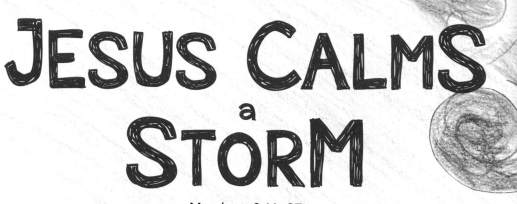

JESUS CALMS a STORM

Matthew 8:16–27

Jesus healed many people in Capernaum. Then he told his disciples he wanted to go to the other side of the Sea of Galilee. So they got into a boat and started across. Out on the lake, a terrible storm hit. A powerful wind blew. Wave after wave swept into the boat.

The disciples were afraid of the storm. But Jesus was sound asleep!

The disciples woke Jesus. "Save us," they cried. They were afraid they were going to die.

Jesus asked, "Why are you afraid, O you of little faith?" Then he stood up and told the wind and the waves to stop. The wind

instantly quieted. The waves stilled. Everything was calm.

The disciples stared at him in amazement. They asked, "What sort of man is this, that even winds and sea obey him?"

FOOD
for
FIVE THOUSAND

Matthew 14:1–21

A ruler named Herod did not want to listen to God's message. He arrested John the Baptist and had him killed. When Jesus heard about John's death, he went off in a boat to a quiet place. But a huge crowd of over five thousand people followed him.

Jesus cared about the people. He healed the sick people who had come to see him. When evening came, the disciples suggested that Jesus send the crowd away to find food.

"They don't need to go away," Jesus told his disciples. "You give them something to eat."

The disciples collected all the food they could find in the crowd. They gave Jesus five loaves of bread and two fish. It seemed impossible to feed so many people with so little food.

Jesus took the food, gave thanks for it, and then handed it to the disciples. They passed out the food to the people. Every person in the crowd ate until they were full. The disciples gathered twelve baskets full of leftovers.

Art by
REYNA
Age 12,
MALAYSIA

173

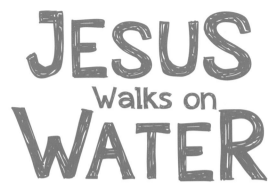

JESUS
Walks on
WATER

Matthew 14:22–36

After Jesus fed more than five thousand people, he went off alone to pray. The disciples got into a boat and planned to meet with Jesus later. But a strong wind made sailing on the Sea of Galilee very difficult.

Late at night, with waves tossing their boat, the disciples saw something on the water. It was Jesus. But he wasn't in a boat. He was walking on the water toward the disciples!

The disciples were scared. They thought the figure walking toward them was a ghost.

Jesus told them, "Do not be afraid."

But Peter wanted proof that this was Jesus. "Lord, if it is you, command me to come to you on the water," Peter said.

Jesus told him to come. Peter stepped out onto the

water, walked, and came to Jesus. When Peter noticed the strong wind, he began to sink.

"Save me," Peter cried.

Jesus reached out his hand to help Peter. "Why did you doubt?" Jesus asked. As soon as they got into the boat, the wind stopped blowing.

"You are the Son of God," the disciples said, and worshiped him.

Art by
ALEX
Age 11,
ITALY

Jesus said that the seed in the story is the word of God. The different soils in the story are like people who hear God's words. The dirt path, where the birds snatched up the seeds, is like people who hear about God, but Satan immediately takes God's word away from them.

Some people are like the rocky ground. They are glad to hear God's words. But then hard times come and right away they give up.

Some people who hear God's words also worry and want to get things. They are like thorny ground. The word is choked out and doesn't take root or produce fruit.

But the good soil is like people who hear God's words, accept them, and bear a lot of fruit.

Art by
JOHN
Age 10,
PHILIPPINES

181

JESUS
Welcomes
CHILDREN

Matthew 18:1–15, 19:13–15; Mark 10:13–15; Luke 18:15–17

One day, the disciples asked Jesus, "Who is the greatest in the kingdom of heaven?"

Jesus pointed to a child. "Whoever humbles himself like this child is the greatest in the kingdom of heaven," he said.

Jesus also added that being kind and welcoming to a child is the same as being kind and welcoming to him.

Another time, many people brought children to meet Jesus. Jesus took them in his arms and blessed them, laying his hands on them. The disciples thought Jesus was too busy to be bothered by children. They told Jesus to make the people take the children away.

But Jesus said, "Let the children come to me." Jesus didn't want his disciples to stop the children. Jesus said that the kingdom of heaven is for those like the children coming to him.

Art by
SILARD
Age 9,
AUSTRALIA

JAIRUS'S DAUGHTER

Mark 5:21–24, 35–43

One day, Jesus sailed across the Sea of Galilee. When he arrived on shore, a crowd surrounded Jesus and his disciples.

A man named Jairus fell down at Jesus's feet. Jairus was a leader of the synagogue, the place where people learned about God.

Jairus told Jesus that his daughter was dying. "Come and lay your hands on her, so that she may be made well and live." His daughter was only twelve years old.

Jesus headed to Jairus's house. On the way, people from Jairus's house came to meet them. "Your daughter is dead," they announced.

But Jesus told Jairus, "Do not fear, only believe." Jesus continued to Jairus's house with Peter, James, and John. When they arrived at the house, they found many people crying.

Jesus asked why the people were crying. "The child is not dead but sleeping," he said.

The people laughed at Jesus.

Jesus sent the people out of the house. Only the child's parents and the three disciples stayed with him. Jesus took Jairus's daughter by the hand and told her, "Little girl, I say to you, get up."

The girl got up and walked. She was alive!

BARTIMAEUS Can SEE!

Mark 10:46–52

Near the city of Jericho, a blind man named Bartimaeus sat by the road begging. He could hear people coming. Jesus and his disciples were leaving the city, followed by a large crowd.

Bartimaeus called out, "Jesus, please help me!"

Some people in the crowd told him to be quiet. But that did not stop Bartimaeus! He kept crying out to Jesus.

Jesus stopped walking and told the people to call the blind man. Bartimaeus left his cloak behind and hurried to Jesus.

"What do you want me to do for you?" Jesus asked.

Bartimaeus told Jesus that he wanted to see.

"Go," Jesus said. "Your faith has made you well."

Bartimaeus was no longer blind. Now he could see, and he followed Jesus on his way.

Art by
SIMŌO
Age 11,
PORTUGAL

The GOOD SAMARITAN

Luke 10:25–37

One day, an expert on the law of Moses asked Jesus how he could get eternal life.

"What is written in the Law?" Jesus asked him.

The man answered, "You shall love the Lord your God with all your heart and with all your soul and with all your strength and with all your mind. And you shall love your neighbor as yourself."

The man had another question for Jesus: "Who is my neighbor?"

To answer this question, Jesus told a parable.

A man who was traveling to Jericho was robbed, beaten, and left for dead. A priest saw him lying on the road, but the priest didn't stop to help him. He continued on his way. A Levite—a helper for a priest—came by. But he didn't help the man either. He continued on his way too.

Art by
BAWOOHANY
Age 12,
MAURITIUS

189

Finally, someone stopped to help the hurt man. The man was a Samaritan. He put bandages on the traveler's wounds. The Samaritan put the man on his animal and took him to an inn. He gave the innkeeper money to take care of the man.

Jesus asked, "Which of these three was a neighbor to the man who fell among the robbers?"

The law expert knew it was the Samaritan. He answered Jesus, "The one who helped him."

"Go," Jesus said, "and do the same kind of thing."

Art by
ISABELLA
Age 12,
NICARAGUA

MARY and MARTHA

Luke 10:38–42

One day, Jesus and his disciples traveled to a small town. A woman named Martha welcomed Jesus into her home.

When Jesus was there, Martha was busy getting food ready for her guests. But her sister, Mary, didn't help. Instead, Mary sat listening to Jesus while he taught. It seemed unfair to Martha that she was doing all the work while Mary did none.

"Lord, don't you care that my sister has left me to serve alone?" Martha complained to Jesus. "Tell her to help me."

Jesus kindly answered her, "Martha, Martha, you are worried and upset about many things, but few things are important. Mary has chosen what is better, and it will not be taken away from her."

The LOST SON

Luke 15:1–2, 11–32

A group of Jewish leaders called Pharisees didn't like that Jesus talked to tax collectors. They thought tax collectors were sinful people.

Then Jesus told them a parable about a man who had two sons. The younger son demanded his inheritance right away, while his father was still alive! Then he headed to a country far away and spent all his money foolishly.

Soon after that, there was a famine in the land. The younger son was starving. He found a job feeding pigs, and he wished he had what the pigs ate. Back home, his father's servants had plenty of food to eat. The son decided to return home. Maybe he could work as a servant in his father's house.

As he got close to home, his father saw him on the road. The father ran to his son and hugged him. He gave his son a ring, a robe, and some shoes. And he threw a party for his son.

The older son was angry about the party. He had stayed home, worked hard, and done what his father had told him to—he was a good son! But his father never had a party for him.

The father told the older son that they should celebrate. He said, "Your brother was lost, and now he is found."

The TEN LEPERS

Luke 17:11–19

Some people were suffering from a bad skin disease called leprosy. These people, called lepers, had to stay away from others so the disease would not spread. The lepers lived outside the cities. Whenever people came near, lepers called out, "Unclean! Unclean!" as the law of Moses told them to do. Then people knew to stay far away.

One day, Jesus came to a village. Ten lepers, who were standing at a distance from Jesus, called out to Jesus. "Jesus, please help us," they said.

Jesus told them, "Show yourselves to the priests." To show themselves to the priest meant that they believed they were healed.

On their way to find the priests,
they realized their leprosy was gone!

Nine of them continued on to find
the priests. But one man turned back,
praising God, to thank Jesus. This man
was a Samaritan.

Jesus asked, "Weren't ten cleansed?
Where are the others? Go on your
way," he said. "Your faith has made
you well."

Art by
MARINA
Age 10,
ARMENIA

ZACCHAEUS

Luke 19:1–10

Zacchaeus was a chief tax collector who lived in Jericho. One day, he heard that Jesus was coming to town!

A large crowd gathered in the streets as Jesus entered the city. Zacchaeus couldn't see over the heads of the people. He was too short. He climbed a sycamore tree and leaned over the branches to see Jesus.

When Jesus walked by the tree, he looked up. "Zacchaeus," he called. "Hurry and come down, for I must stay at your house today."

Zacchaeus hurried down. He was happy to have Jesus in his home. The people in the crowd grumbled about Jesus going to stay with a tax collector. People disliked tax collectors because they worked for the Roman government. Sometimes they took more money than needed and kept it for themselves.

Zacchaeus told Jesus that he would give half of what he owned to the poor. He also said that if he had cheated anyone, he would give that person back four times what he took.

Art by
MIRA
Age 9,
EGYPT

Jesus told the crowd that he had come to save those who had
done wrong things.

LAZARUS
Returns to
LIFE

John 11:1–44

Jesus had a dear friend named Lazarus, the brother of Mary and Martha, who lived in the town of Bethany. One day, Lazarus became very sick. Mary and Martha sent a message to Jesus, telling him that Lazarus was sick. But Jesus stayed where he was for two days.

By the time Jesus arrived in Bethany, Lazarus was already dead and buried.

"If you had been here," Martha cried, "my brother would not have died. But even now I know that whatever you ask from God, God will give you."

Jesus told her Lazarus would come back to life. But Martha didn't understand what he meant.

Mary came to see Jesus. She cried about Lazarus. Jesus cried too. A group of people went to Lazarus's tomb, where Jesus said, "Take away the stone."

Lazarus had been in the tomb four days. Martha said the smell would be bad. But the people obeyed Jesus and moved the stone that covered the tomb.

Jesus prayed, then called, "Lazarus, come out."

Suddenly, Lazarus came out of the tomb, still wrapped in burial linen cloths! He was alive!

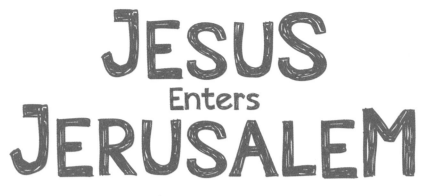

JESUS
Enters
JERUSALEM

Matthew 20:17–19; 21:1–11

I t was time to go to Jerusalem to celebrate the Passover. Jesus had been to Jerusalem many times before. But this time was different. He told his disciples that soon he was going to die.

Before Jesus entered the city, he gave two disciples instructions. He told them to find a donkey with her colt. If anyone asked them what they were doing, they were to say, "The Lord needs them."

The disciples brought the animals back to Jesus. They put their cloaks on the donkeys for Jesus to ride. Hundreds of years before this happened, God had told the prophet Zechariah, "Behold, your king is coming to you, humble, and mounted on a donkey, on a colt." And that's how Jesus entered Jerusalem.

A crowd gathered in the road. They greeted Jesus the way they would greet a great person. Many people spread branches from trees on the road. Others spread their cloaks in the road. They called out, "Hosanna to the Son of David. Blessed is he who comes in the name of the Lord!"

Some people wondered who Jesus was. Others answered, "This is the prophet Jesus, from Nazareth of Galilee."

CAST OUT
of the
TEMPLE

Mark 11:15–18

The temple in Jerusalem was a place where people came from near and far to worship the God of Israel. In the temple, they could buy animals for offerings. People from far away could trade the coins of their country for the coins used in Jerusalem.

When Jesus arrived in Jerusalem, he went into the temple. Right away, he saw people buying and selling things.

Jesus knocked over the tables of the money changers. He knocked over the chairs of the people selling pigeons. Jesus forced the buyers and sellers to leave the temple. "Is it not written, 'My house should be called a house of prayer for all the nations'?" Jesus said. "But you have made it a den of robbers."

People were amazed by what Jesus said. But the priests and other leaders in Israel were afraid. They wanted to find a way to put Jesus to death.

The LAST SUPPER

John 13–17

During the Passover meal, Jesus got up from the table and wrapped a towel around his waist. He filled a bowl with water and began washing the disciples' dirty feet.

Peter didn't want Jesus to wash his feet. That was the job of a servant. But Jesus continued anyway. He explained that if he, their teacher, was willing to wash their feet, then they must be willing to wash one another's feet. Jesus washed their feet as an example to teach them how to treat other people.

While they ate, Jesus was upset. "One of you will betray

me," he said to his disciples. "It is the person I give this piece of bread to." He gave the bread to Judas, and Judas left. But the other disciples did not understand what Judas planned to do.

During the meal, Peter promised that he would never betray Jesus. He said he would be willing to die for Jesus. But Jesus had bad news for Peter. He said, "Before the rooster crows, you will have denied me three times."

Jesus told his disciples that he would be going away soon, but that he would send the Holy Spirit to be with them. He spent the last of his time with his disciples teaching them and praying for them.

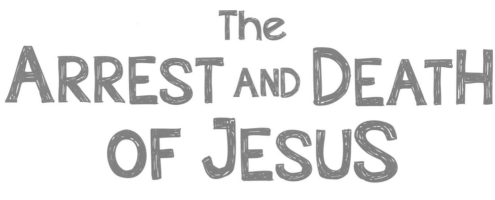

The ARREST AND DEATH OF JESUS

Matthew 26:36–27:66

After the Passover meal, Jesus and his disciples went to a garden called Gethsemane. It was night. Jesus was very sad, so he prayed to God. He asked his disciples to wait with him while he prayed, but they fell asleep.

Soon a mob of people arrived, led by Judas. He greeted Jesus with a kiss, which was a signal for some men to arrest Jesus. The disciples ran away.

Jesus was taken to the high priest and other leaders in Jerusalem. They would decide what to do with him. Some people told lies about Jesus. But Jesus did not defend himself.

Peter followed Jesus and waited outside. Someone recognized Peter as one of Jesus's disciples, but Peter said, "I do not know what you mean." Just as Jesus said, Peter denied knowing Jesus three times that night.

The high priest asked Jesus if he was the Messiah, the Son of God. Jesus answered, "You have said so."

This made the high priest and the rest of the leaders angry. They wanted Jesus to be put to death. They sent him to Pilate, the Roman governor.

Art by
JIMWELL
Age 11,
PHILIPPINES

Pilate asked Jesus if he was the King of the Jews. Jesus answered, "You have said so."

Pilate didn't think Jesus should be put to death, but he didn't want to upset the people. Every year at Passover, one prisoner was allowed to go free. Pilate asked the people who they wanted to free—a criminal named Barabbas, or Jesus.

The crowd shouted, "Barabbas."

"What shall I do with Jesus?" Pilate asked.

"Let him be crucified!" the people cried.

The soldiers whipped Jesus and put a crown made of sharp thorns on his head. They led him to a place outside Jerusalem called Golgotha. There he was nailed to a cross between two criminals. The people shouted insults at him. Some of Jesus's friends watched sadly from a distance.

The sky grew dark from noon until three o'clock. Jesus cried out, "My God, my God, why have you forsaken me?"

Jesus cried out again, and then he died. Suddenly, the ground shook. The curtain in the temple tore in two. The Roman soldiers were amazed at what they saw. One said, "Truly this was the Son of God!"

A man named Joseph asked for Jesus's body and buried him. Roman soldiers guarded the huge stone in front of the tomb to make sure no one stole Jesus's body.

Art by
JIMWELL
Age 11,
PHILIPPINES

The
RESURRECTION

John 20:1–18

Mary Magdalene was a friend and follower of Jesus. On the first day of the week after Jesus had been buried, she went to his tomb early, while it was still dark. But when she got there, she saw that the stone in front of the tomb had been rolled to the side.

Mary quickly found Peter and John and told them what she had discovered. They ran to the tomb and looked inside. They found the linen cloths that had been wrapped around Jesus. But they didn't find a body in the tomb. Where was Jesus?

Peter and John returned home. But Mary Magdalene stayed at the

Art by
MAXIMILIAN
Age 9,
GERMANY

tomb. She was crying. When she peeked inside, she saw two angels sitting
where Jesus's body had been.

"Why are you weeping?" they asked.

"They have taken away my Lord," Mary said. Suddenly, she noticed a man standing behind her. She thought he was the gardener.

Mary asked him where Jesus's body might be, and he responded, "Mary."

Now she recognized who he was—Jesus!

Mary soon spread the news. She had seen Jesus! He was alive again!

Art by
CHRIS
Age 12,
CANADA

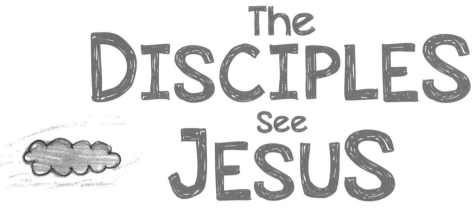

The
DISCIPLES
See
JESUS

John 20:19–21:25

It was the evening of the first day of the week after Jesus was crucified and buried. The disciples met together in a house. They had locked the doors. Even so, Jesus appeared in the room!

"Peace be with you," he said. He showed them his wounds to prove that he had truly returned to life.

Thomas was not with the disciples then. When he heard that Jesus was alive, Thomas didn't believe it. But eight days later, Jesus appeared when Thomas was with the disciples.

Jesus showed Thomas the nail marks in his hands. "Do not disbelieve, but believe," said Jesus.

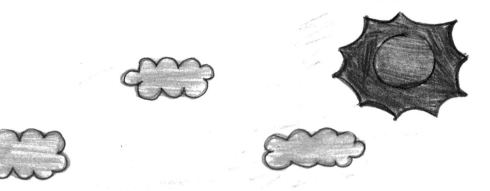

The disciples saw Jesus many times after that. One day, seven of the disciples went fishing together. But they didn't catch any fish.

A man on the shore told them to throw their net on the right side of the boat.

Soon they caught so many fish, they couldn't pull the net into the boat. Now they knew who the man was—Jesus!

Peter jumped into the water and swam back to shore. Then they all ate breakfast with Jesus.

Art by
RATCHUMAS
Age 9,
THAILAND

The HOLY SPIRIT COMES

Acts 1–2

After his death and resurrection, Jesus appeared to many people. For forty days, he showed that he was alive. He taught about the kingdom of God. Then the time came for Jesus to return to heaven.

Jesus told his disciples not to leave Jerusalem. "You will be baptized with the Holy Spirit, and you will receive power when the Holy Spirit has come upon you."

Suddenly, Jesus was lifted up into the sky. The amazed disciples watched until he was hidden by a cloud.

Two angels appeared nearby. "Why do you stand looking into heaven?" they asked. "This Jesus will come in the same way as you saw him go into heaven."

Days later, people came from all over to celebrate Pentecost, the Jewish Festival of Weeks. At this festival, the people gave thanks for the harvest. The disciples and others had gathered in a room. Suddenly, they heard a rushing wind. Something that looked like a flame appeared on each person. The Holy Spirit had come! Jesus's followers started speaking in languages they had never spoken before. The people listening were amazed and confused. They could understand everything in their own languages.

Peter preached a message about Jesus. About three thousand people believed Peter's message and were baptized.

Art by
CASIMIRO
Age 9,
NICARAGUA

HEALING
at the
GATE

Acts 1:4–5, 3:1–16

During Jesus's life, his disciples saw him do many amazing things. But then Jesus returned to heaven. Before he left, Jesus told the disciples that the Holy Spirit would give them power to do amazing things too. His words came true.

Peter and John headed to the temple one afternoon. On the way, they saw a man being carried to one of the temple gates. Since this man couldn't walk, he begged for money in the same place each day.

The lame man asked Peter and John for money.

"I have no silver and gold," said Peter. "But what I do have, I give to you. In the name of Jesus Christ of Nazareth, rise up and walk!"

Immediately the man's feet and ankles became strong. He jumped up and began to walk. He leaped for joy and praised God.

The people who saw were amazed. Peter told everyone that faith in the name of Jesus had healed the man.

219

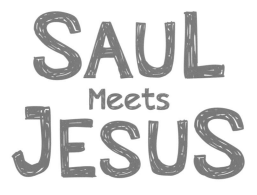

SAUL
Meets
JESUS

Acts 9:1–31

Saul was a Jew who wanted to stop people from preaching about Jesus. He went to the high priest of the temple to get permission to put followers of Jesus in prison in Jerusalem.

While he was on the way to the city of Damascus one day, a bright light from heaven surrounded Saul. He fell to the ground. He heard a voice say, "Saul, Saul, why are you persecuting me?"

"Who are you, Lord?" Saul asked.

"I am Jesus. Get up and go into the city. You will be told what to do," said the voice.

Suddenly, Saul was totally blind! He had to be led into the city.

Saul waited in the city for three days, without eating or drinking. Then God spoke to a man named Ananias through a special dream called a vision. He told Ananias to find Saul and heal him.

Ananias was confused. Saul was an enemy to the people who followed the teachings of Jesus! But Ananias obeyed God. He went to Saul and placed his hands on him. Saul could see again!

Saul stopped arresting the followers of Jesus. Instead, he believed in Jesus and began to preach about him. He became known as Paul, his Roman name.

Art by
CHANTELLE
Age 9,
MAURITIUS

PETER and DORCAS

Acts 9:36–43

One of Jesus's followers was a woman named Tabitha. She was also called Dorcas. She lived in a town called Joppa.

Dorcas did many things to help poor people. But one day, Dorcas got sick and died. The people in Joppa were sad, because Dorcas had helped so many people.

Some of the followers of Jesus asked Peter to come to Joppa and help.

When Peter arrived, he went upstairs to the room where Dorcas's body lay. A group of widows had gathered in the room, and they were crying. They showed Peter the clothes Dorcas had made.

Peter sent everyone out of the room. Then Peter prayed and said, "Tabitha, arise."

The dead woman opened her eyes! She was alive! Peter showed her to the widows. Soon everyone in town had heard about this miracle, and many people believed in Jesus.

Peter ESCAPES from PRISON

Acts 12:1–19

King Herod began to hurt some of the followers of Jesus. He had Peter arrested and put in prison. Peter was kept in chains and guarded by sixteen soldiers. The followers of Jesus prayed for Peter to be released.

The night before Peter's trial, he was suddenly awakened. The prison cell was full of light.

An angel stood in his cell! "Get up quickly," the angel said. The chains fell off Peter. "Dress yourself and put on your sandals."

Peter did what he was told. But he thought he was having a dream.

The angel led Peter right past the guards and outside the prison. The city gate opened by itself! Then, suddenly, the angel disappeared. Now Peter knew this was not a dream. He hurried to a friend's house and knocked on the door.

Many people were inside praying for Peter. A servant girl named Rhoda went to the door. But when she heard Peter's voice, she ran back to tell the others without letting Peter in!

Rhoda told the others that Peter was outside.

They didn't believe her, but Peter kept knocking. When they opened the door, Peter told them how God had freed him from prison.

Art by
FAWZY
Age 12,
EGYPT

SHIPWRECKED!

Acts 27:1–28:16

Paul preached about Jesus for many years. Later, he was arrested in Jerusalem and put on trial. Paul asked to speak to the emperor in Rome. Julius, a Roman soldier, took Paul and other prisoners on a boat to Rome.

They set sail before winter set in. After much time had passed, the sailing became dangerous since winter was about to begin. Paul warned Julius that a disaster would happen if they kept going. But he didn't listen to Paul.

A strong wind turned into a storm. The sailors threw the ship's cargo overboard, hoping to keep going. But the storm grew so bad, many thought they would die.

An angel of the Lord appeared to Paul one night during the storm. Paul told his shipmates part of the angel's message.

"Take heart, no one will die," he warned, "but the ship will be destroyed."

Art by
FRANCESCO
Age 11,
ITALY

Soon they spotted land—the island of Malta. The ship was torn apart. But everyone—all 276 people—made it safely to shore, just as the angel had said. On the island, Paul was bitten by a snake. Everyone thought he would die, but he lived! Paul also healed people on the island who were sick. Later, Paul and the others set sail on another ship to Rome.

A HEAVENLY CITY

Revelation 1:9, 21:1–22:21

While he was on the island of Patmos, John had a vision of a new heaven and earth.

John saw a shining city called the new Jerusalem coming down from the sky. It had a wall with twelve gates. Jewels sparkled from the wall. The streets were made of gold.

A voice from the throne of God told John that this is where God would live with his people forever.

"He will wipe away every tear from their eyes, and there will be no more death," the voice said. "There will be no more mourning, or crying, or pain anymore."

In the city, there was no need for the light from the sun or moon. All the light came from God. And there was no more night. A river ran down the middle of the city. It was the water of life, flowing out of the throne of God. And the tree of life stood on both sides of the river.

At the end of John's vision, Jesus said, "I am coming soon."

Art by
JAN
Age 11,
CROATIA

ABOUT THE ART

This storybook Bible has some amazing art! And every piece of art inside the book was drawn by a young reader between the ages of eight and twelve. Do you want to know how we collected the art?

We invited young artists in countries around the world to be a part of this fun and interesting project. We shared Bible stories and asked them to pick their favorite stories to illustrate. We collected more than seven hundred drawings from more than fifty countries! Then we went through all the drawings and picked those that worked best in the book. There were so many great illustrations to choose from—we wish we could have used more. But we wanted to represent as many countries as we could, and we had limited space in the book.

On the next two pages, you will see a map that shows all of the countries that the art came from.

COUNTRY MAP

Argentina
Armenia
Australia
Bangladesh
Belarus
Bolivia
Brazil
Canada
China
Colombia
Croatia
Dominican
  Republic
Egypt
Ethiopia
Georgia
Germany

Greece
Guatemala
India
Indonesia
Italy
Japan
Madagascar
Malawi
Malaysia
Mali
Mauritius
Mexico
Moldova
Montenegro
Nepal
Nicaragua
Nigeria

Pakistan
Philippines
Portugal
Russia
Serbia
Singapore
South Africa
Sri Lanka
Thailand
Ukraine
United Arab
  Emirates
United Kingdom
United States
Venezuela

CANADA

UNITED STATES

MEXICO

DOMINICAN
REPUBLIC

GUATEMALA

NICARAGUA

VENEZUELA

COLOMBIA

BRAZIL

BOLIVIA

ARGENTINA

UNITED
KINGDOM

BELARUS

GERMANY UKRAINE

CROATIA MOLDOVA

SERBIA

ITALY MONTENEGRO GEORGIA

PORTUGAL GREECE ARMENIA

RUSSIA

CHINA

JAPAN

PAKISTAN NEPAL

BANGLADESH

EGYPT INDIA

UNITED ARAB PHILIPPINES
EMIRATES

THAILAND

MALI

NIGERIA ETHIOPIA SRI LANKA MALAYSIA

SINGAPORE

INDONESIA

MALAWI

MADAGASCAR MAURITIUS

AUSTRALIA

SOUTH
AFRICA

PEOPLE AND PLACES INDEX

Art by
COLTER
Age 9,
UNITED
STATES

Art by
JOVANA
Age 12,
MONTENEGRO

Art by MARIAM Age 11, GEORGIA

museum of the Bible

EXPERIENCE THE BOOK
THAT SHAPES HISTORY

Museum of the Bible is a 430,000-square-foot building located in the heart of Washington, D.C.—just steps from the National Mall and the U.S. Capitol. Displaying artifacts from several collections, the Museum explores the Bible's history, narrative, and impact through high-tech exhibits, immersive settings, and interactive experiences. Upon entering, you will pass through two massive, bronze gates resembling printing plates from Genesis 1. Beyond the gates, an incredible replica of an ancient artifact containing Psalm 19 hangs behind etched glass panels. Come be inspired by the imagination and innovation used to display thousands of years of biblical history.

Museum of the Bible aims to be the most technologically advanced museum in the world, starting with its unique Digital Guide that allows guests to personalize their museum experience with navigation, customized tours, supplemental visual and audio content, and more.

For more information and to plan your visit, go to
museumofthe**Bible**.org.